NURTURING YOUR WRITING CALM

CORALEE A. NELSON &
MARGUERITE JANE JONES

admin@ThePublishingCircle.com
or
THE PUBLISHING CIRCLE, LLC
Regarding: Coralee A. Nelson or Marguerite Jane Jones
19215 SE 34th Street
Suite 106-347
Camas, WA 98607

FIRST EDITION
ISBN: 978-1-947398-29-0

NURTURING YOUR WRITING CALM /
CORALEE A. NELSON & MARGUERITE JANE JONES

Cover & interior book design & icons by Michele Uplinger
Cover painting © Janet Hendershot, and used by permission of the artist

Nurturing Your Writing Calm

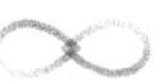

This book will help you develop a writing practice that assists you in achieving your writing goals, while supporting you so you can overcome blocks that get in the way of your writing momentum.

Dedication

CORALEE DEDICATES this book to her supportive hubby and sons; and to her loving parents, one who resides in heaven and the other who is still on earth. I love you all!

JANE DEDICATES this book to her four children, who have filled her life with love, inspiration, and encouragement. I love each of you!

To serendipity
that resulted in our meeting,
and the conversations
that made us friends and creative collaborators

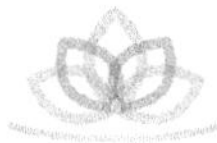

TABLE OF CONTENTS

Welcome

Welcome to *Nurturing Your Writing Calm.* The book you hold in your hands is truly unique. The *Nurturing Your Writing Calm (NYWC)* process outlined here, is dedicated to helping you develop a daily ten-minute writing practice that will assist you in meeting your long-term writing goals.

At the heart of *Nurturing Your Writing Calm* is a desire to inspire you to nurture a powerful connection with your truest self through the simple practice of daily writing. *Nurturing Your Writing Calm* has been thoughtfully designed, with specific elements woven throughout the book, to bring you to a place of peace and inspiration geared to stimulate your deepest creativity and stir your motivation.

The art and finesse of writing is a passion and pastime for many people. While many enjoy writing, even more wish they were writers. When you pick up a pen and sit with this process, you become a writer. Welcome, writer!

Nurturing Your Writing Calm invites you to quiet your mental and emotional distractions so you can write. The daily practices teach your nervous system to rest, and then you are ushered into a writing aventure that will arouse your genius and talent so you can accomplish your writing goals.

Nurturing Your Writing Calm facilitates getting in touch with your physical senses, emotions, and life experiences that are full of ingenious potential. As a result of using this daily ten-minute writing practice, you'll feel more powerful. Using this book, you will see your creativity abound and your interest in writing peak. Your motivation will increase through the 365 days. Don't worry! You strengthen your abilities all along the way; it doesn't take a full year to embrace the expanded version of yourself. The calming strategies, setups and starters will be there to gently support and inspire you as you write.

Writing using the *Nurturing Your Writing Calm* approach becomes an adventure when you enter a relaxed state that helps you overcome any writing blocks and then moves you to connect with your own imagination in a deeply personal manner.

The structure of *Nurturing Your Writing Calm* is simple. Each day, you will find two sets of directions that, combined, bring you to a place of calm creativity. The first is a calming strategy and the second is a writing prompt that is composed of a setup and starter. You might be inclined to skip the calming strategy because all you want to do is write. However, being in a calm-alert state is known to enhance inspiration, quiet the voices of stress, and better integrate your brain's hemispheres so you can have a more "whole-brain" writing experience.

How
Nurturing Your Writing Calm
Will Benefit You

The *Nurturing Your Writing Calm* process is built into this book. It helps you explore your writing abilities, dive deep into your own imaginative potential, and build a writing practice that results in you meeting your writing goals.

Taking time to calm your nervous system comes with more benefits than simply developing a sustainable daily writing practice. Calming your nervous system is linked to less anxiety and a better mood. Supporting the habit of creating a calm inner place gives you tools that can be used throughout your day to create peace when you need it most. Quelling the voices of stress and anxiety opens your mind for creativity in writing as well as in other parts of life. Thinking on your feet, being present in relationships, accessing learned information more easily, completing daily "to-do" lists, engaging in more confident decision making, and sleeping better at night are all associated with teaching your nervous system to be calm in a recurring manner.

The *Nurturing Your Writing Calm* process is a powerful balm for the stresses of daily life, leaving you feeling more balanced. Opening your mind to build images, characters, feelings, and sensations creates energy and motivation that helps you accomplish your goals. Even the accomplishment of small goals, such as writing for five minutes a day, sparks feelings of success.

The Key Vehicles
of
Nurturing Your Writing Calm

The Vehicle of Ten Minutes a Day

THE FRENETIC PACE OF modern, western life tends to be taxing. Therefore, carving out a manageable amount of time in which to write is necessary. For *Nurturing Your Writing Calm* purposes, a time frame of ten minutes is short enough to entice writers to write every day. Finding ten minutes within a twenty-four-hour period is attainable for most people and does not result in the overwhelmed feeling that can come with adding an additional daily task.

To sustain the flexibility inherent in the *Nurturing Your Writing Calm,* consider these time-frame options when seeking to plan your daily practice of ten minutes. They include:

- Getting up ten minutes earlier

- Using one's breaktime at work to write

- Writing while waiting for dinner to cook

- Using ten minutes before getting ready for bed

Writing ten minutes every day provides the vehicle for developing a sustainable, creative writing practice that will begin to clarify and help you rediscover or re-define your own writing goals. It is not always realistic to have a specific time designated for writing. Being flexible with the time-frame results in the ability to enter the calming practice for five minutes before writing productively within a full ten-minute time frame.

Whether you are an aspiring writer who has an unexplained aversion to writing, or an established writer who has faced writer's block as an expected part of the writer-rhythm, you can transform your reality.

Each calming strategy is chosen and repeated for two weeks in order to gain some mastery. It is used with a daily creative writing prompt (setup and starter). Together, these support your experience with your own imagination. The *Nurturing Your Writing Calm* provides the perfect frame to introduce and sustain a beneficial writing practice.

The Vehicle of a Daily Practice

VARIOUS PERSPECTIVES EXIST with respect to cultivating habit-forming practices. *Nurturing Your Writing Calm process* uses a daily routine to help writers develop a lifestyle writing habit. These habits are formed in response to individual intentions and diligent application of a skill that affects how people routinely live their lives.

From a theoretical perspective, daily routines are universally acknowledged as habits for successful transformation. According to tradition, transformation has four stages: renewal, repair, regeneration, and rebirth. Notice the process indicated is growth oriented without undue strain.

Writers often make conscious and unconscious decisions about writing because of the influences they encounter in life. The decisions are frequently limiting and rooted in fear. These self-induced restrictions can cause frustration and angst, even at a subliminal level, resulting in aversion to writing, writer's block, or procrastination.

Decisions tend to be made at formative stages of development and progress into beliefs that sometimes hinder growth and expression. This is often the case with writer's block or procrastination about writing.

The purpose of the *Nurturing Your Writing Calm* process is to gently address through practice, your individual attitudes about writing. The *Nurturing Your Writing Calm* book helps you build a writing practice that is simple, brief, and allows you the freedom to enter a new writing space. Both the calming strategies and the creative writing prompts reduce the voices of pessimism that may get in the way of your writing.

When you decide to incorporate the *Nurturing Your Writing Calm* process and start your writing practice, decisions that created limitations or boundaries are subtly encountered, and a new awareness opens you to a fresh writing reality. What you may find surprising is that your hidden abilities surface and can be readily accessed.

The *Nurturing Your Writing Calm* book is designed with simple, easy to remember and follow calming strategies with unique creative writing setups and starters to stimulate your senses and encourage you to write every day. This book assists in the process of releasing restrictive decisions and shepherding you into a practice that is rejuvenating and impactful.

The Vehicle of Calming Strategies

THE CALMING STRATEGIES in *Nurturing Your Writing Calm* are specifically aimed at preparing you for writing. With our driven, task-focused, and stress-filled lives it can be hard to focus on those things we say we want to do, like being creative and innovative—things like writing.

Five minutes is allotted for the calming-strategy section. Take your time to read the strategy and understand the process. For your ease, you will observe they are written to include some similar elements.

Notice if you sigh, swallow, or yawn. These responses may indicate your system has entered a state of rest and are signals that you are ready to move on to the writing portion. Not every calming strategy requires a full five minutes, but don't rush and inadvertently miss the benefits.

You may not be aware that there is an ideal state for creativity. Rather, you may push yourself to be artificially creative, effectively stalling the generation of imagination. You may have determined you lack creativity because you are not easily able to enter the ideal state. Or maybe you substitute a formula for your own creativity, denying your innate ability by taking direction from others.

Nevertheless, while you may not be able to explain creativity, you may recognize it when you see or experience it. Writers know they are "in the zone" but are not always clear about how to get there. Researchers have come to describe the state when learning and creativity emerges as the *calm-alert* or *relaxed-alert* state. This is where the imagination is invited to be involved in the joyful pursuit of dreaming, visioning, and innovating.

When your nervous system is *calm-alert*, the mind is available for learning or imaginative pursuits. The calming strategies are intended to bring you into the calm-alert state by incorporating counting, rhythm, sensory attunement, and somatic strategies in harmony with the breath. A noticeable level of the calm-alert state is typically reached quite quickly when the calming strategies are practiced and sustained. You may choose to use calming strategies throughout the course of the day, resulting in greater benefits.

There are numerous reasons that you may avoid entering creative awareness. Time is often cited as one such reason. "Writer's block" is another reason you may give for not engaging in a writing practice. The more subtle reason, however, is often that creativity involves becoming open and vulnerable. You may shield yourself from becoming exposed to avoid the possibility of being disappointed. Also, you may feel like not trying is better than trying and failing. These inner struggles often provoke an uncertainty that prevents you from engaging in the very thing that will help move you forward.

Stress is one of the biggest inhibitors of creative imagination. Maladaptive stress creates a biochemical response that can hinder innovation and imagination. When too much adrenaline and cortisol are triggered by stress, the prefrontal cortex or the thinking part of the brain is compromised. During stress, the nervous system keeps the brain in an alarmed state so it can be on guard to protect itself. This keeps the brain from being able to work at full capacity.

The alarm system that triggers stress is designed to keep you safe from those things that can harm. Unfortunately, this threat-awareness system responds similarly when you swerve to miss a dog dashing across the street or when ruminating about all the work piling up at the office, the laundry that needs folding, the car that should be taken into the mechanic, the bills that need to be paid, or a relationship that is causing upset.

The alarm system responds to all these things by alerting you to "danger." When you are in a state of chronic stress, there is a tendency to dodge the very thing you may say you want. In this case, it is to write. The *Nurturing Your Writing Calm* strategies help to hush the noise of the world. Once the noise settles, you can explore and enjoy your creativity.

Unfortunately, writing often evolves into a stress-filled experience through a developmental process that leaves the love of writing wanting. For example, you may describe that you did not feel safe in school because your imagination was constrained and directed by the "system of education." As a child, maybe you were told to sit in a chair or at a desk and write with letters formed a certain way. Maybe you were taught to value "getting it right." Being compliant is typically attached to acceptance. The Western way of "doing school" teaches that conformity matters and creative mediocrity is safer than innovative brilliance. In school, situations that made you feel insecure or out of control may have developed into stress-filled reminders that continue to impact your ability to generate thoughts and tap into your creativity even now.

Two calming strategies are provided per thirty-day period. It is beneficial to experience both calming strategies within each period. Consider using a calming strategy for two weeks and then moving to the next one.

Read each calming strategy thoroughly, as some are more technical than others. This does not mean they are difficult. Reading each calming strategy and understanding the progression prior to your first attempt will ensure you benefit the most from each and every calming strategy.

The Vehicle of the Declaration

THE BRIDGE BETWEEN the calming strategy and the setup is a declaration. This declaration is designed to safely usher your creative writing into a space of calm that reduces inhibitions that once got in the way. These are short, affirmative, and believable statements that are not threatening.

This part of the practice is unique in that it clarifies the transition points between the vehicles. This ensures maximum benefit from the ten minutes: the calming strategies, the setups, and starters. As a result, the vehicle of a daily writing routine establishes momentum toward building your writing goals.

With consistent use, the calming strategies, declarations, setups, and starters provide the opportunity for the brain to equate safety with creativity. The multiple benefits of integrating creative writing and the calming strategy include using the declaration to produce the bridge to access your creative abilities. Once engaged, your internal environment takes center stage. Creative imagination now has the capacity to flourish.

The Vehicle of the Creative Writing Prompts

THE CREATIVE WRITING PROMPTS are based on the Pebbling Process™. There are two parts to the creative writing prompts. The first step is the setup and the second is the starter.

Each setup and starter will subtly link you with your own imagination. The setup and starter are vital connections to access and follow your creative urge and are incorporated seamlessly after the calming strategy.

The setup follows the declaration, which rides on the heels of the calming strategy. Once the setup has been experienced using the senses, the starter is introduced, bringing you, the writer, to the page for your personal style of expression.

To do this, the setup creates a scene in your awareness that engages your senses and stokes your imagination to bring thoughts and feelings into the present moment. You may or may not have experiences related to the setup. The setup does not give any specific direction regarding writing; it simply provides a tap into your imagination before the starter is read. Once you have read the setup, the next step is to set a timer for five minutes, read the starter, and begin writing. The flow of writing comes readily and pulls directly from your creativity—your truest writing self.

To be clear, the *Nurturing Your Writing Calm* setup is different from many traditional prompts individuals are familiar with. It is not intended that you write about the setup; rather that your creative mind be engaged in a scene that can be experienced.

The starter steers you into the process of bringing your imagination easily to the page. Just as the declaration at the end of the calming strategy brings your creative writing into a space of peace, the starter brings your writing into your now active imagination.

The starter provides a short phrase, part of a thought, a picture, or an experience to initiate your daily writing practice. It is intended that the starter gently allow your imagination to go in a direction all its own. Putting your pen to the page, you write the words following the phrase, "Begin writing with . . ." and continue until your timer says the five minutes is over.

Example
Creative Writing Setup (five minutes)

> Searching for a memory, his heart beats a familiar rhythm. He blinks to the day before: the glove on his hand, the ball slamming into it as he stood in mid-field, the rush as the ball reached the third baseman's glove. The runner was out and they were so proud of him! One more blink as the memory vanishes, and he's back in the present.

Creative Writing Starter

> *Opening the rusty gate . . .*

It is important to stop writing when five minutes is over. When the timer chimes, lift your pen from the page—there's no need to finish the word, thought, or sentence. Lifting your pen mid-word or mid-sentence may feel a bit uncomfortable at first, but you will soon be used to it.

Stopping in the middle of a creative thought or idea does not stop your creativity. As you complete your *Nurturing Your Writing*

Calm practice for the day, your creative imagination carries on. Performing this small but significant action in the *Nurturing Your Writing Calm* process deepens your experience of a connection with your own creative ability. It quickly becomes easier for you to write than not write. You will find yourself engaging the calming strategies with greater intention and awareness as an integral part of your writing practice.

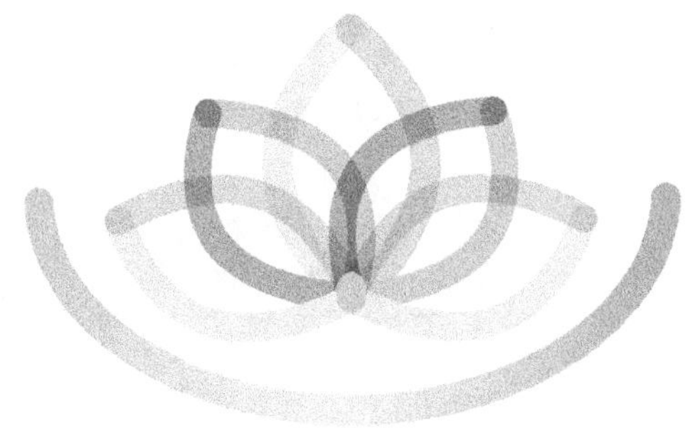

GETTING STARTED

NELSON / JONES

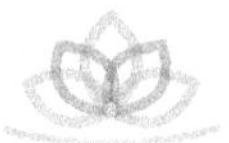

Getting Started

THE FOLLOWING ARE STRATEGIES you may find beneficial as you begin your own *Nurturing Your Writing Calm* process.

- Choose your start date—today or tomorrow would be good.

- Select a pen, blank paper or journal for your daily writing.

- Choose a writing space that is as free of distractions as possible, placing your pen and paper at the ready.

- Track your progress daily.

It is ideal to plan an early morning writing time and space before your day becomes busy. Five minutes of calming with five minutes of writing is easier the first thing in the morning before your day becomes busy. If something happens to interrupt your writing time, you have the rest of the day to find the necessary ten minutes.

It is helpful to take a few minutes the night before and have your writing materials set out in an accessible place. On days when morning writing is not possible, you may consider taking your writing with you.

About Your Pen

IT MIGHT BE SURPRISING to find a discussion about pens in *Nurturing Your Writing Calm.* In fact, the comfort, ease, and flow of a pen contribute substantially to a positive and engaging writing experience. Below are considerations for choosing a pen.

- Select a pen before you sit to write.

- Make sure it has ink in it—while this seems obvious it's often overlooked. A depleted pen will interrupt your writing.

- Ensure the pen doesn't skip, leak, or pool; this will spoil your writing experience.

- Choose a pen that feels good in your hand.

- Consider trying a different color of ink, as it enriches your experience as you write.

Select a pen that feels comfortable in your hand. Creativity will flow more freely onto the page when using a pen that writes smoothly and has a color of ink you are happy with.

Your Timer

LIKE PENS, A TIMER is a useful tool. Both the calming strategy and the writing portion are split into five-minute segments.

- Use a timer that will allow for five-minute time segments, totaling ten minutes in all. (There are multiple timer apps for both your smartphone and computer.)

- A standard kitchen timer works well; be sure you like the ticking sound before purchasing one.

- Stopwatches are not useful for timing yourself unless you have someone helping.

Select a timer that is convenient and easy to use. In addition, choose a timer that is accessible and possibly transportable if you are traveling.

About Your Writing Page

A BLANK PAGE can be daunting and unfamiliar when first encountered, but it is full of potential. The more comfortable you are with the blank page, the more possibilities you can explore. Select an unlined writing page, allowing your imagination freedom.

Now that you are organized with your pen and timer at hand, you are ready to experience the *Nurturing Your Writing Calm* practice in its full effect.

A Note to Lefties

IF YOU ARE A LEFTIE who was discouraged and made to write with your right hand, *Nurturing Your Writing Calm* is an opportunity to return to your natural writing hand. Please be encouraged to consider using your left hand and see what happens for you.

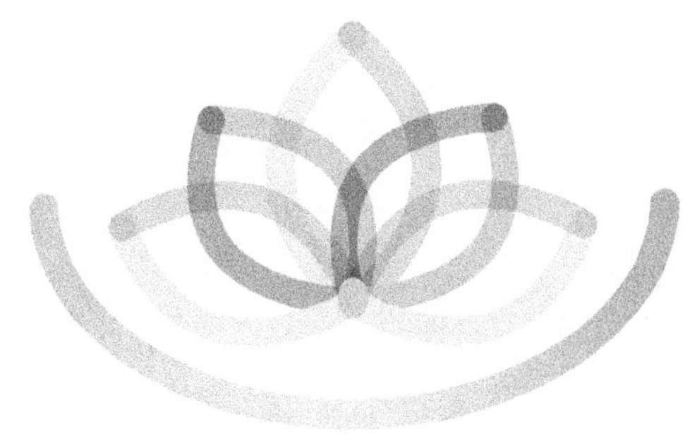

CALMING STRATEGIES

Nurturing Your Writing Calm

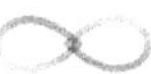

Calming Strategy One

SIT IN A QUIET, comfortable place with soothing lighting and few, if any, interruptions.

Close your eyes and gently set aside any mental and emotional concerns or distractions.

Slowly take a deep belly breath by breathing in through your nose while your abdomen expands, then exhale through your mouth while your abdomen contracts.

Take your time and notice what you are sitting on, how it feels to your body. Is the surface soft or hard? Let your body sink into your seat and become comfortable as you sit.

Again, take your time and notice your feet resting on the floor; notice how the floor feels under your feet. Is it warm or cool? Let your feet sink into the floor and notice how every part of your foot touches the floor.

Take another slow, deep belly breath by breathing in through your nose while your abdomen expands, then breathe out slowly through your mouth while your abdomen contracts.

Gently open your eyes and look to the ceiling without lifting your chin. Let your eyes settle on the spot you have found and rest your cupped hand on the crown of your head.

Notice how you feel in your body, how you are sitting, and how your feet are resting. Notice if you swallow, sigh, or yawn.

Complete another deep belly breath by breathing in through your nose while your abdomen expands, then breathe out slowly through your mouth while your abdomen contracts.

Say out loud or to yourself, "I am ready to write."

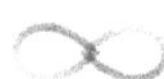

Calming Strategy Two

SIT IN A QUIET, comfortable place with soothing lighting. Find a spot where you'll experience few, if any, interruptions.

Close your eyes and gently set aside any mental and emotional concerns or distractions. Tell your distractions you will be back later to address them after you have focused on your daily writing practice.

Slowly take a deep belly breath by breathing in through your nose while your abdomen expands, then breathe out slowly through your mouth while your abdomen contracts.

Moving your focus to your hands, bring your two index fingers together under your nose and above your upper lip. Tap on this spot gently in 4/4 rhythm. This is the typical rhythmic pattern one hears in classic rock songs. Emphasize the first beat of the rhythm by tapping stronger on **1.**

   1 - 2 - 3 - 4   **1** - 2 - 3 - 4   **1** - 2 - 3 - 4
   1 - 2 - 3 - 4   **1** - 2 - 3 - 4

Maintain a slow and steady, comfortable rhythm.

Continue tapping with your eyes closed and return your focus to your breathing.

Slowly open your eyes and look to the ceiling without lifting your chin. Rest your cupped hand on the crown of your head.

Notice how you feel. Take note of a sigh, swallow, or yawn.

Now take another deep belly breath by breathing in through your nose while your abdomen expands, then breathe out slowly through your mouth while your abdomen contracts.

Say out loud or to yourself, "My mind and emotions are available for creativity."

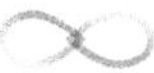

Calming Strategy Three

SIT IN A QUIET, comfortable place with soothing lighting and few, if any, interruptions.

Close your eyes and gently set aside any mental and emotional concerns or distractions.

Slowly take a deep belly breath by breathing in through your nose while your abdomen expands, then intentionally exhale through your mouth while your abdomen contracts.

Notice how sitting in your quiet comfortable place has already started to move you into a state of calm.

While continuing to belly breathe, open your eyes.

Notice and identify the numerous colors and shades in the room. Become aware of the scents in the room. Become aware of the temperature and hear any subtle sounds.

Enter the space you reside in fully, allowing your senses to overtake your worries, thoughts, or mental intrusions. Be present here in your place, mindfully experiencing your five senses to the degree you are able in the five minutes allotted.

Lift your eyes to the ceiling without lifting your chin and rest your cupped hand lightly on the crown of your head.

Notice how you feel. Take note of a swallow, sigh, or yawn.

Complete one more deep belly breath by breathing in through your nose while your abdomen expands, breathe out slowly through your mouth while your abdomen contracts.

Say out loud or to yourself "I am in the present; I am prepared to write."

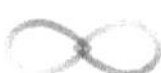

Calming Strategy Four

SIT IN A QUIET, comfortable place with soothing lighting and few, if any, interruptions.

Close your eyes and gently set aside any mental and emotional concerns or distractions.

Slowly take a deep belly breath by breathing in through your nose while your abdomen expands, then exhale through your mouth while your abdomen contracts.

Notice how sitting in your quiet, comfortable place has already started to move you into a state of calm.

While continuing to belly breathe, open your eyes.

Using your right hand, tap your right thigh. Using your left hand, tap your left thigh.

Alternate back and forth for eight counts (use a 4/4 rhythm, with emphasis on beat number **1**).

Move your hands to your chest. Tap your hands at the same time on your chest, right below your collarbone, for eight counts.

Using your right hand, tap your right thigh. Using your left hand, tap your left thigh. Alternate back and forth for eight counts.

Move your hands to your chest. Tap your hands at the same time on your chest, right below your collarbone, for eight counts. And so on.

Slowly open your eyes and look to the ceiling without lifting your chin. Rest your cupped hand on the crown of your head.

Notice how you feel and take note of a swallow, sigh, or yawn.

Pay attention to your breathing and complete another deep belly breath by breathing in through your nose while your abdomen expands, then breathe out slowly through your mouth while your abdomen contracts.

Say out loud or to yourself, "Writing is natural, like my breath."

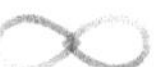

Calming Strategy Five

SIT IN A QUIET, comfortable place with soothing lighting and few, if any, interruptions.

Close your eyes and gently set aside any mental and emotional concerns or distractions.

Slowly take a deep belly breath by breathing in through your nose while your abdomen expands, then breathe out slowly through your mouth while your abdomen contracts.

Cross your hands over your chest, grasp right below your shoulders, and squeeze gently. Say in your mind "1, 2, 3, 4; relax, 2, 3, 4." Relax your grip on the word "relax," squeeze again when you start "1, 2, 3, 4."

1, 2, 3, 4; relax, 2, 3, 4.

1, 2, 3, 4; relax, 2, 3, 4.

1, 2, 3, 4; relax, 2, 3, 4.

Complete a comfortable number of cycles of squeezing and relaxing, saying, "1, 2, 3, 4; relax, 2, 3, 4."

Slowly open your eyes and look to the ceiling without lifting your chin. Rest your cupped hand on the crown of your head.

Notice how you feel and take note of a swallow, sigh, or yawn.

Pay attention to your breathing and complete another deep belly breath by breathing in through your nose while your abdomen expands, then breathe out slowly through your mouth while your abdomen contracts.

Say out loud or to yourself, "I look forward, with anticipation, to my daily writing."

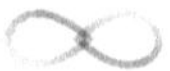

Calming Strategy Six

IF YOU CAN, LIE in a quiet, comfortable place with soothing lighting and few, if any, interruptions.

Close your eyes and gently set aside any mental and emotional concerns or distractions.

Slowly take a deep belly breath by breathing in through your nose while your abdomen expands, then exhale through your mouth while your abdomen contracts. Take three deep belly breaths, exhaling longer each time.

Feel yourself relaxing more with each breathe. As you exhale say in your mind or out loud, "I am calm."

Keep belly breathing and place your hand below your belly button, feeling your belly rise and fall with each breath.

Each time you exhale, declare an "I" or "my" statement that resonates with you about your writing. Consider one of these phrases:

"I am creative."

"I am innovative."

"I am inspired."

"I am free to experience possibilities."

"My writing helps me explore opportunities."

"My inner creative world is full of potential."

When you have completed at least three statements while belly breathing, gently open your eyes. Let your eyes settle on the spot you have found and rest your cupped hand on the crown of your head.

Unhurriedly sit up. Notice how you feel in your body, how you are sitting, and how your legs and feet are positioned. Notice if you swallow, sigh, or yawn.

Complete another deep belly breath by breathing in through your nose while your abdomen expands, then breathe out slowly through your mouth while your abdomen contracts.

Say out loud to yourself, "I am interested to see how my creativity is expressed today."

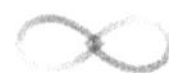

Calming Strategy Seven

SIT IN A QUIET, comfortable place with soothing lighting and few, if any, interruptions.

Close your eyes and gently set aside any mental and emotional concerns or distractions.

Slowly take a deep belly breath by breathing in through your nose while your abdomen expands, then breathe out through your mouth while your abdomen contracts.

Gently place your fingers just below your collarbone and tap gently in a 4/4 rhythm. Tap more prominently on **1**, 2, 3, 4. Allow your rhythm to be slow and steady, emphasizing the **1** on each set of four counts.

Once you have a comfortable rhythm established without much thought, cross your hands over your chest. Keep tapping **1**, 2, 3, 4; **1**, 2, 3, 4.

Uncross your hands and continue tapping **1**, 2, 3, 4; **1**, 2, 3, 4 with a steady and slow pace.

Cross your hands and continue tapping **1**, 2, 3, 4; **1**, 2, 3, 4.

Uncross your hands and continue tapping **1**, 2, 3, 4; **1**, 2, 3, 4 using a steady and slow pace. Continue for as long as is comfortable with the timeframe of five minutes.

Notice how you feel. Take note of when you swallow, sigh or yawn.

Slowly open your eyes and look to the ceiling without lifting your chin. Rest your cupped hand on the crown of your head.

Complete another deep belly breath by breathing in through your nose while your abdomen expands, then breathe out slowly through your mouth while your abdomen contracts.

Say out loud to to yourself, "My imagination will take me to new places today."

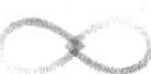

Calming Strategy Eight

SIT IN A QUIET, comfortable place with soothing lighting and few, if any, interruptions.

Close your eyes and gently set aside any mental and emotional concerns or distractions.

Slowly take a deep belly breath by breathing in through your nose while your abdomen expands, then exhale through your mouth while your abdomen contracts. Take three deep belly breaths, exhaling longer each time.

Recall a time when you were inspired by a stirring experience. Perhaps you were stimulated by the work of an artist or musician, by a breathtaking natural vista, or an original design. If no experience comes to mind, imagine one that would be inspirational.

Picture that experience in vivid detail. Bring to mind the various visual elements that are salient to you. Experience them in full color, texture and shape.

Notice sounds that existed in that experience of inspiration. Pay attention to the pitch, tone, rhythm or volume of the sounds present there.

Recall the smells you experienced during your memorable time. Bring them to mind, engaging your olfactory senses, causing the event to come alive in your present space.

Keep breathing deeply, focusing on your exhale while maintaining a vibrant recollection of your inspired experience as you continue to belly breathe.

Gently open your eyes and look to the ceiling without lifting your chin. Let your eyes settle on the spot you have found and rest your cupped hand on the crown of your head.

Notice how you feel in your body, how you are sitting, and how your body is relaxed. Notice if you swallow, sigh, or yawn.

Say out loud or to yourself, "Beauty and ingenuity is all around me; it's mine for the taking."

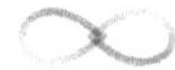

Calming Strategy Nine

SIT IN A QUIET, comfortable place with soothing lighting and few, if any, interruptions.

Close your eyes and gently set aside any mental and emotional concerns or distractions.

Slowly take a deep belly breath by breathing in through your nose while your abdomen expands, then exhale through your mouth while your abdomen contracts. Take three deep belly breaths, exhaling longer each time.

Notice your shoulders. Shrug and rotate them until they feel looser.

With your fingers, find your jaw joint on both sides of your face. Gently massage your jaw while opening and closing your mouth without strain.

As you inhale, open your mouth incrementally wider. Notice the back of your throat and open it as you inhale, allowing air to stream into your throat. Finish your yawning inhale with a sigh or a huff.

Return your breathing to a belly breath. Do so by breathing in through your nose while your abdomen expands, then breathe out slowly through your mouth while your abdomen contracts.

Gently open your eyes and look to the ceiling without lifting your chin. Let your eyes settle on the spot you have found and rest your cupped hand on the crown of your head.

Notice how you feel in your body, how you are sitting and how your feet are resting. Notice if you swallow, sigh, or yawn.

Complete another deep belly breath by breathing in through your nose while your abdomen expands, then breathe out slowly through your mouth while your abdomen contracts.

Say out loud or to yourself, "Engaging creatively is pleasurable for me."

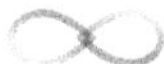

Calming Strategy Ten

PRIOR TO BEGINNING, find a blank sheet of paper and a pen or pencil that flows easily when you write. Place them in front of you on a table or desk.

Sit in a quiet, comfortable place with soothing lighting and few, if any, interruptions.

Close your eyes and gently set aside any mental and emotional concerns or distractions.

Slowly take a deep belly breath by breathing in through your nose while your abdomen expands, then exhale through your mouth while your abdomen contracts. Take three deep belly breaths, exhaling longer each time.

Pick up your writing utensil. On your blank page, begin by drawing two to four simple shapes—hearts, circles, squares, stars, moons, ovals or a combination. Then, simply doodle among them, within and near the shapes. Do not critique or overthink your doodling.

Allow your mind to relax with your continued belly breathing. Doodling frees your mind to be at rest when there is no expectation or required outcome. Doodle for up to five minutes.

When five minutes is up, put your writing utensil down. Roll your shoulders back, smile a small smile and look to the ceiling without lifting your chin. Let your eyes settle on the spot you have found and rest your cupped hand on the crown of your head.

Notice how you feel in your body, how you are sitting, and how your body is relaxed. Notice if you swallow, sigh, or yawn.

Say out loud or to yourself, "Invention flows freely through my hand."

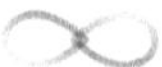

Calming Strategy Eleven

SIT IN A QUIET, comfortable place with soothing lighting and few, if any, interruptions.

Close your eyes and gently set aside any mental and emotional concerns or distractions.

Slowly take a deep belly breath by breathing in through your nose while your abdomen expands, then breathe out through your mouth while your abdomen contracts.

Place your fingers just below your collarbone and tap gently in 4/4 rhythm.

Tap more prominently on **1**, 2, 3, 4. Allow your rhythm to be slow and steady, emphasizing the **1** on each set of four counts.

Once you have a comfortable rhythm established without much thought, return to focus on your breathing. Continue tapping while you belly breathe.

Notice how you feel. Take note of when you swallow, sigh, or yawn.

Slowly open your eyes and look to the ceiling without lifting your chin. Rest your cupped hand on the crown of your head.

Slowly complete another deep belly breath by breathing in through your nose while your abdomen expands, then breathe out slowly through your mouth while your abdomen contracts.

Say out loud or to yourself, "I notice that being calm and writing have an interesting interplay."

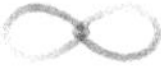

Calming Strategy Twelve

SIT IN A QUIET, comfortable place with soothing lighting and few, if any, interruptions.

Close your eyes and gently set aside any mental and emotional concerns or distractions.

Slowly take a deep belly breath by breathing in through your nose while your abdomen expands, then exhale through your mouth while your abdomen contracts. Take three deep belly breaths, exhaling longer each time.

Cross your arms over your chest and place your fingers about four fingers' width below your armpit (for women, on your bra line). At a steady pace, begin tapping in four-four rhythm, with more emphasis on the **one count.** Count **1**, 2, 3, 4, four times as you tap gently under both arms.

This is a typically rhythmic pattern one hears in classic rock song. Emphasize the first beat of the rhythm by tapping stronger on **1.** Maintain a slow, steady and comfortable rhythm.

Once you have completed sixteen counts, uncross your arms and move your hands to your chest, an inch or so below the collarbone. Shift your hands toward your shoulders slightly and a couple of inches below your collarbone. With your fingers formed like a beak, tap solidly for sixteen counts, with more emphasis on the **one count.** Count **1**, 2, 3, 4, four times to reach sixteen counts.

Complete the same pattern of tapping gently under the arms for sixteen counts.

Uncross your arms and move to your chest, tapping more solidly for four sets of four counts, emphasizing the **one count.**

Gently drop your hands to your side and complete another deep belly breath by breathing in through your nose while your abdomen expands. Then, breathe out slowly through your mouth while your abdomen contracts.

Say out loud or to yourself, "My body is at rest and I have all the resources I need to create."

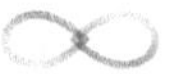

Calming Strategy Thirteen

SIT IN A QUIET, comfortable place with soothing lighting and few, if any, interruptions.

Close your eyes and gently set aside any mental and emotional concerns or distractions.

Slowly take a deep belly breath by breathing in through your nose while your abdomen expands, then exhale through your mouth while your abdomen contracts. Take three deep belly breaths, exhaling longer each time.

Recall a time when you relished a creative venture. Perhaps you were painting, sculpting, writing, singing, dancing or decorating. If no experience comes to mind, imagine one that would be enjoyable and meaningful.

Picture that experience in vivid detail. Bring to mind the various visual elements that are salient. Experience them in full color, texture and shape.

Notice sounds that existed in that experience. Pay attention to the pitch, tone, rhythm or volume of the sounds present there.

Recall the smells you experienced during your memorable creative time. Bring them to mind, engaging your olfactory senses, causing the event to come alive in your present space.

Keep breathing deeply, focusing on your exhale and maintaining a vibrant recollection of your creative space while belly breathing.

Gently open your eyes and look to the ceiling without lifting your chin. Let your eyes settle on the spot you have found and rest your cupped hand on the crown of your head.

Notice how you feel in your body, how you are sitting, and how your body is relaxed. Notice if you swallow, sigh, or yawn.

Say out loud or to yourself, "Creativity has always been a part of me and continues to this day."

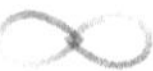

Calming Strategy Fourteen

SIT IN A QUIET, comfortable place with soothing lighting and few, if any, interruptions.

Close your eyes and slowly take a deep belly breath by breathing in through your nose while your abdomen expands. Then exhale through your mouth while your abdomen contracts.

Take your index, second and third fingers and place them, stacked one on the other, above the curve of your eyebrows. Pull the skin taut across your forehead and apply light pressure.

While pressing lightly on your forehead, take a deep belly breath by breathing in through your nose while your abdomen expands, then breathe out slowly through your mouth while your abdomen contracts. Count to four on the inhale and then four on the exhale.

Should you notice any stressors, worries or concerns, don't push them away, but hold them loosely as you continue pressing on your forehead with your fingers. Continuing to press lightly on your forehead and pulling the skin taut, take a deep belly breath by breathing in through your nose while your abdomen expands, then breathe out slowly through your mouth while your abdomen contracts. Count to five on the inhale and five on the exhale.

Now count to six on the inhale and six on the exhale.

Gently open your eyes and look to the ceiling without lifting your chin. Let your eyes settle on the spot you have found and rest your cupped hand on the crown of your head.

Notice how you feel in your body, how you are sitting, and how your feet are resting. Notice if you swallow, sigh, or yawn.

Complete another deep belly breath by breathing in through your nose while your abdomen expands, then breathe out slowly through your mouth while your abdomen contracts.

Say out loud or to yourself, "Daily writing brings me joy."

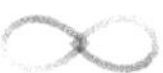

Calming Strategy Fifteen

SIT IN A QUIET, comfortable place with soothing lighting and few, if any, interruptions.

Close your eyes and gently set aside any mental and emotional concerns or distractions.

Slowly take a deep belly breath by breathing in through your nose while your abdomen expands, then exhale through your mouth while your abdomen contracts. Take three deep belly breaths, exhaling longer each time.

Notice your shoulders. Shrug and rotate them until they feel looser. Notice your hands; gently shake them to loosen the fingers.

Starting with your right hand, use your left hand to massage your thumb on either side of your nail bed. Massage for a few seconds. Move to your index finger and use your left hand to massage on either side of your nail bed. Massage for a few seconds. Move to your middle finger and so on until you have finished massaging your right hand's fingers. Finally move to the fleshy part on the outside of your palm and massage that area for a few seconds.

Moving to your left hand, use your right to massage your thumb on either side of your nail bed. Massage for a few seconds. Continue massaging around your fingers, focusing on either side of the nail bed and finishing with the fleshy part on the outside of your palm.

Complete another deep belly breath by breathing in through your nose while your abdomen expands, then breathe out slowly through your mouth while your abdomen contracts.

Say out loud or to yourself, "My mind and hands are prepared to write."

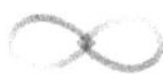

Calming Strategy Sixteen

SIT IN A QUIET, comfortable place with soothing lighting and few, if any, interruptions.

Close your eyes and gently set aside any mental and emotional concerns or distractions.

Slowly take a deep belly breath by breathing in through your nose while your abdomen expands, then exhale through your mouth while your abdomen contracts. Take three deep belly breaths, exhaling longer each time.

Close your eyes. Notice how your spine sits atop your tailbone. See a straight and strong spine in the center of your back.

Now, imagine your vertebrae being gently stacked one on the other, protecting the life force of the spinal cord and the essential spinal nerves within. With each belly breath imagine the spinal column being built from your tailbone to your brain stem. Imagine a strong, straight and long spinal column that protects an essential part of your central nervous system, your spinal cord.

Gently open your eyes and look to the ceiling without lifting your chin. Let your eyes settle on the spot you have found and rest your cupped hand on the crown of your head.

Notice how you feel in your body, how you are sitting, and how your feet are resting. Notice if you swallow, sigh, or yawn.

Complete another deep belly breath by breathing in through your nose while your abdomen expands, then breathe out slowly through your mouth while your abdomen contracts.

Say out loud or to yourself, "My inner strength supplies me with fresh, new insight."

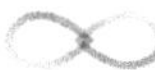

Calming Strategy Seventeen

SIT IN A QUIET, comfortable place with soothing lighting and few, if any, interruptions.

Close your eyes and gently set aside any mental and emotional concerns or distractions.

Take a deep belly breath and focus your attention on your breath. Slowly breathe in through your nose while your abdomen expands, then breathe out slowly through your mouth while your abdomen contracts.

Remember a writing prompt that produced a positive writing experience.

While continuing to belly breathe, recall **emotions** you felt.

While continuing to belly breathe, recall **thoughts** you had.

While continuing to belly breathe, recall any **excitement** experienced.

While continuing to belly breathe, invite your senses into that time and place, and experience your writing through your senses.

Notice how you feel. Take note of when you swallow, sigh, or yawn.

Slowly open your eyes and look to the ceiling without lifting your chin. Rest your cupped hand on the crown of your head.

Slowly complete another deep belly breath by breathing in through your nose while your abdomen expands, then breathe out slowly through your mouth while your abdomen contracts.

Say out loud or to yourself, "I am being impacted by my daily writing."

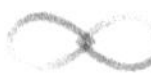

Calming Strategy Eighteen

SIT IN A QUIET, comfortable place with soothing lighting and few, if any, interruptions.

Close your eyes and gently set aside any mental and emotional concerns or distractions.

Slowly take a deep belly breath by breathing in through your nose while your abdomen expands, then exhale through your mouth while your abdomen contracts. Take three deep belly breaths, exhaling longer each time.

With eyes still closed, place your middle finger on the inside of your eyebrow on your brow bone. Extend your index finger across to the outside of your eyebrow and settle that finger on that end of your brow bone.

With gentle pressure, slowly massage in a clockwise direction. Complete about five rotations. Then, increase the pressure slightly and continue to massage in a clockwise direction, completing about five rotations. Increase the pressure slightly one more time and circle clockwise for about five rotations.

Remove your hands and take a deep belly breath by breathing in through your nose while your abdomen expands, then exhale through your mouth while your abdomen contracts.

Replace your fingers on your eyebrow, with your middle finger on the center and index finger on the outside of the brow bone. As you have already done, complete three sets of five rotations, increasing the pressure slightly with each rotation cycle. This time, complete the rotations in a counter-clockwise fashion.

Gently open your eyes and look to the ceiling without lifting your chin. Let your eyes settle on the spot you have found and rest your cupped hand on the crown of your head.

Notice how you feel in your body, how you are sitting, and how your legs are relaxed. Notice if you swallow, sigh, or yawn.

Complete another deep belly breath by breathing in through your nose while your abdomen expands, then breathe out slowly through your mouth while your abdomen contracts.

Say out loud or to yourself, "Daily writing draws me into a place of calm innovation."

Calming Strategy Nineteen

SIT IN A QUIET, comfortable place with soothing lighting and few, if any, interruptions.

Close your eyes and gently set aside any mental and emotional concerns or distractions.

Slowly take a deep belly breath by breathing in through your nose while your abdomen expands, then exhale through your mouth while your abdomen contracts. Take three deep belly breaths, exhaling longer each time.

Recall a place where you have experienced nervous system rest. The place could be the beach, in a forest, on a mountain or at the home of a dear friend. Any place where you find your worries and cares are reduced or eliminated.

Picture that location in vivid detail. Bring to mind the various visual elements that are salient. See them in full color, texture and shape.

Notice sounds that reside in that location. Pay attention to the pitch, tone, rhythm or volume of the sounds present there.

Notice smells you have experienced in that location. Bring them to mind, engaging your olfactory senses, causing the location to come alive in your present space.

Keep breathing deeply, focusing on your exhale and maintaining a vibrant recollection of your calming place while belly breathing.

Gently open your eyes and look to the ceiling without lifting your chin. Let your eyes settle on the spot you have found and rest your cupped hand on the crown of your head.

Notice how you feel in your body, how you are sitting, and how your body is relaxed. Notice if you swallow, sigh, or yawn.

Say out loud or to yourself, "My life experiences are rich and full, guiding me to write with liberty."

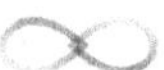

Calming Strategy Twenty

SIT IN A QUIET, comfortable place with soothing lighting and few, if any, interruptions.

Close your eyes and gently set aside any mental and emotional concerns or distractions.

Slowly take a deep belly breath by breathing in through your nose while your abdomen expands, then exhale through your mouth while your abdomen contracts. Take three deep belly breaths, exhaling longer each time.

Close your eyes. Notice your feet on the floor. Then pay special attention to your calves. Pay attention to the fact that the muscles give strength to your legs.

Flex your calves gently for about five seconds and then relax them. Notice relief in relaxing.

Take a deep belly breath.

Move your focus back to your calves and flex them gently for about five seconds and then relax them. Notice the relief in relaxing.

Take a deep belly breath.

Complete one or two more cycles of flexing and relaxing your calves.

Gently open your eyes and look to the ceiling without lifting your chin. Let your eyes settle on the spot you have found and rest your cupped hand on the crown of your head.

Notice how you feel in your body, how you are sitting, and how your legs are relaxed. Notice if you swallow, sigh, or yawn.

Complete another deep belly breath by breathing in through your nose while your abdomen expands, then breathe out slowly through your mouth while your abdomen contracts.

Say out loud or to yourself, "My creativity is a natural extension of myself."

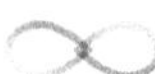

Calming Strategy Twenty-One

SIT IN A QUIET, comfortable place with soothing lighting and few, if any, interruptions.

Close your eyes and gently set aside any mental and emotional concerns or distractions.

Slowly take a deep belly breath by breathing in through your nose while your abdomen expands, then exhale through your mouth while your abdomen contracts. Take three deep belly breaths, exhaling longer each time.

Place the fingers of both hands on the U between your collarbone. Then using both hands, move them about an inch toward your shoulders. Gently massage that area and move toward your shoulders, massaging lightly on spots that are sore.

Put your right palm on your breastbone. Put your left hand on your bellybutton with fingers spread. Hold both positions, using soft pressure.

Breathe in through your nose to the count of four, and exhale to the count of four, holding your breastbone and bellybutton positions softly.

Now breathe in through your nose to the count of four, and exhale to the count of five, holding your breastbone and bellybutton positions softly.

Next, breathe in through your nose to the count of four, and exhale to the count of six, holding your breastbone and bellybutton positions softly.

Finishing, breathe in through your nose to the count of six, and exhale to the count of six, holding your breastbone and bellybutton positions softly.

Gently open your eyes and look to the ceiling without lifting your chin.

Let your eyes settle on the spot you have found and rest your cupped hand on the crown of your head.

Notice how you feel in your body, how you are sitting, and how your feet are resting. Notice if you swallow, sigh, or yawn.

With hands in a comfortable position, complete another deep belly breath by breathing in through your nose while your abdomen expands, then breathe out slowly through your mouth while your abdomen contracts.

Say out loud or to yourself, "Daily writing continues to transport me to novel places."

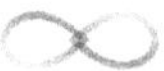

Calming Strategy Twenty-Two

SIT IN A QUIET, comfortable place with soothing lighting and few, if any, interruptions.

Close your eyes and gently set aside any mental and emotional concerns or distractions.

Slowly take a deep belly breath by breathing in through your nose while your abdomen expands, then exhale through your mouth while your abdomen contracts. Take three deep belly breaths, exhaling longer each time.

Take your right hand and gently massage the soft webbed spot between your left index finger and thumb. Massage in a clockwise direction ten rotations, then counterclockwise ten rotations.

Then moving to the outside of your right hand below the pinky finger on the fleshy part, rub gently.

Next, find a point three finger-widths below the wrist. On that point, press and circle in a clockwise direction and then in a counterclockwise direction for ten rotations.

Take your left hand and gently massage the soft spot between your right index finger and thumb. Massage in a clockwise direction ten rotations, then counterclockwise ten rotations.

Repeat the massage directions on your left hand.

Roll your shoulders back and gently shake out your hands in front of you.

If your eyes are still closed, open them and look to the ceiling without lifting your chin.

Let your eyes settle on the spot you have found and rest your cupped hand on the crown of your head.

Notice how you feel in your body, how you are sitting, and how your feet are resting. Notice if you swallow, sigh, or yawn.

Complete another deep belly breath by breathing in through your nose while your abdomen expands, then breathe out slowly through your mouth while your abdomen contracts.

Say out loud or to yourself, "There is wonder to be expressed through my writing today."

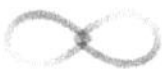

Calming Strategy Twenty-Three

FIND A QUIET, COMFORTABLE place with soothing lighting and few, if any, interruptions.

If you are able, lie down on your back with your arms comfortably at your sides, palms up. Close your eyes and gently set aside any mental and emotional concerns or distractions.

Slowly take a deep belly breath by breathing in through your nose while your abdomen expands, then exhale through your mouth while your abdomen contracts. Take three deep belly breaths, exhaling longer each time.

Pay attention to your spine as it rests on the ground. Imagine a straight line running from the back of your head, down to your sacrum. As you breathe, imagine your spine lengthening and straightening without force or strain.

Continuing your belly breaths, turn your hands toward your thighs and tap the side of your right thigh, then your left thigh. Tap approximately sixteen times back and forth between your thighs.

Let your mouth curve gently into a smile.

Gently open your eyes and look at the ceiling. Let your eyes settle on the spot you have found and rest your cupped hand on the crown of your head, then tap gently on your head.

Notice how you feel in your body. Notice if you swallow, sigh, or yawn.

Complete another deep belly breath by breathing in through your nose while your abdomen expands, then breathe out slowly through your mouth while your abdomen contracts. Sit up slowly.

Say out loud or to yourself, "I am confident; I am at peace."

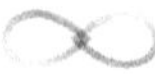

Calming Strategy Twenty-Four

FIND A QUIET, COMFORTABLE place with soothing lighting and few, if any, interruptions.

If you are able, lie down on your back with your arms comfortably at your sides, palms up. Close your eyes and gently set aside any mental and emotional concerns or distractions.

Slowly take a deep belly breath by breathing in through your nose while your abdomen expands, then exhale through your mouth while your abdomen contracts. Take three deep belly breaths, exhaling longer each time. Notice how your breathing is affecting your thought processes. Smile gently.

Place your hands on your stomach and take a deep belly breath. Focus your attention on your breath.

Slowly breathe in through your nose while your abdomen expands.

Breathe out through your mouth while your abdomen contracts.

Notice how your back pushes into the floor when you breathe in. Smile gently.

Return focus to your hands on your stomach and take a deep belly breath. Notice your attention on your breath.

Open your eyes and look to the ceiling without lifting your chin. Using either hand, place your cupped hand on the back side of your head, resting your hand lightly in that area. Notice that part of your head.

Slowly take a deep belly breath by breathing in through your nose while your abdomen expands, then exhale through your mouth while your abdomen contracts. Take three deep belly breaths, exhaling longer each time.

Say out loud or to yourself, "My writing is meaningful to me."

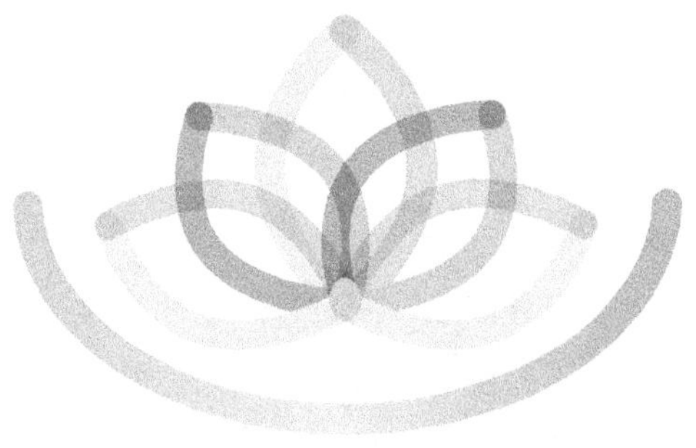

365 DAYS
of
Calm
Creative Writing

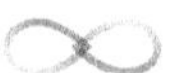

Day One
Select Calming Strategy One or Two

Creative Writing Setup One

Searching for a memory, his heart beats a familiar rhythm. He blinks to the day before: the glove on his hand, the ball slamming into it, as he stood in mid-field, the rush as the ball reached the third baseman's glove. The runner was out and they were so proud of him! One more blink and the memory vanishes and he's back in the present.

Creative Writing Starter One

Begin writing with: Opening the rusty gate . . .

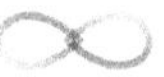

Day Two
Select Calming Strategy One or Two

Creative Writing Setup Two

See yourself sliding your feet into thick, itchy, wool socks while wiggling your toes as you pull them up as high as they will go, first your right foot, then your left. "Ah, what's this?" A big toe is peeking through a tiny hole that was not there yesterday. Pulling the sock over and tucking it in under and between your toes, you slide your foot into the boot. "It's a little hole, I'll mend it another day."

Creative Writing Starter Two

Begin writing with: From behind the . . .

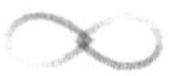

Day Three
Select Calming Strategy One or Two

Creative Writing Setup Three

Visualize picking your way along rain-slicked cobblestone streets to where hot drinks and warm cakes are served to tables filled with people in quiet conversations. As you reach another corner you stop, look up, and confusion sets in. The smell of coffee, fresh sweets, and breads fill the air, but where is the smell coming from? Someone says, "Hello, my friend. You do not see me?" Turning, your friend's smile greets you from a bistro table across the street.

Creative Writing Starter Three

Begin writing with: Locks on the . . .

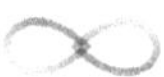

Day Four
Select Calming Strategy One or Two

Creative Writing Setup Four

The swollen wood of the window frame, covered with layers of peeling white paint, causes the window to resist being pushed out from its winter position into the cool spring morning. Finally, the frame gives way, opening to the morning songbirds and the warmth of the sun cresting the horizon.

Creative Writing Starter Four

Begin writing with: Through the rush of . . .

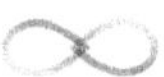

Day Five
Select Calming Strategy One or Two

Creative Writing Setup Five

As he shifted his weight to confirm it was safe, the ladder creaked its warning. Taking another step, he peered into the attic space that held time. He looked down into the old woman's waiting eyes, as she anticipated the trunk she sent him to find. Casting the flashlight about, he caught sight of the brass lock and buckles. The trunk that held her life, her journals and her letters, was soon in her hands.

Creative Writing Starter Five

Begin writing with: Yellow lamplight . . .

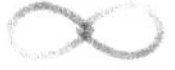

Day Six
Select Calming Strategy One or Two

Creative Writing Setup Six

Wrapping your sweater closer as you shiver, your knees rub together like a cricket, and you pull your morning coffee close. You gaze through the rising steam to the thick rain streaming down the window. With a sigh you reach for the phone.

Creative Writing Starter Six

Begin writing with: Lifting her pen . . .

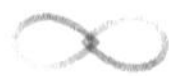

Day Seven

Select Calming Strategy One or Two

Creative Writing Setup Seven

Remember how it feels to be in that moment between being asleep and awake, when your breath pauses, and you ponder whether to drift back to sleep or rouse yourself fully awake? The morning sounds draw your breath up, and you wake.

Creative Writing Starter Seven

Begin writing with: Damp forest . . .

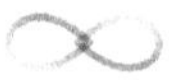

Day Eight

Select Calming Strategy One or Two

Creative Writing Setup Eight

There's a splintering crash of fine china as it hits the stone floor of the dining room, then silence. You jolt from bed in an instant. The continued silence causes your heartbeat to quicken and sharpens your hearing. Your hands and feet gingerly feel their way down the hall.

Creative Writing Starter Eight

Begin writing with: Thin curtains hung . . .

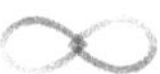

Day Nine
Select Calming Strategy One or Two

Creative Writing Setup Nine

You sit upright on the embroidered bench, your feet ready at the pedals, your hands still and suspended above the yellowed ivory keys. Silence. Then there's a nod and a tip of the conductor's wand. Music fills the air.

Creative Writing Starter Nine

Begin writing with: Like broken wheels . . .

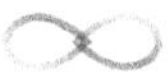

Day Ten
Select Calming Strategy One or Two

Creative Writing Setup Ten

On her toes, peering through the peephole, she saw they were looking around, setting down the weight of their bags. They rang again and knocked. She waited, watching them. Soon one of them pressed their eye to the outside of the peephole, trying to see if she was at home. She then opened the door. That was her favorite part of their visits.

Creative Writing Starter Ten

Begin writing with: From the top . . .

Day Eleven
Select Calming Strategy One or Two

Creative Writing Setup Eleven

Standing in their flannel pajamas, feet bare, full of expectations, they bunched together as the snow fell outside the window. Shivering, they pressed their faces against the glass to get closer to the snow.

Creative Writing Starter Eleven

Begin writing with: A knock at the door . . .

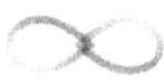

Day Twelve
Select Calming Strategy One or Two

Creative Writing Setup Twelve

Riding over cobblestone streets, past night-shuttered windows, the bicycle clattered and bounced as its rider pushed them both forward. The bike could not know its rider's anticipation of the baking breads, pastries and sweets, but it did know it was being propelled forward in keen eagerness.

Creative Writing Starter Twelve

Begin writing with: Six milk jugs . . .

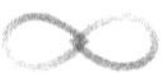

Day Thirteen
Select Calming Strategy One or Two

Creative Writing Setup Thirteen

They were a mile away from the morning noise, yet they heard the traffic building in waves like the tide coming in. They closed their eyes, imagined the ocean mist on their faces, and enjoyed their time together.

Creative Writing Starter Thirteen

Begin writing with: Young oak trees . . .

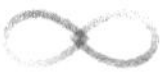

Day Fourteen
Select Calming Strategy One or Two

Creative Writing Setup Fourteen

The water in the creek bed was running a little faster than usual. Lying on the bridge with their eyes searching the shallow places with their fishnets ready, they had high hopes some tadpoles would venture out.

Creative Writing Starter Fourteen

Begin writing with: Runners on the path . . .

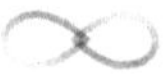

Day Fifteen
Select Calming Strategy One or Two

Creative Writing Setup Fifteen

Trying to read scribbled directions as the car bounced over bumps and dropped in and out of potholes made their trip longer than it needed to be. Turning down a side street, they were greeted by a dozen balloons tied to a white picket fence. They had arrived.

Creative Writing Starter Fifteen

Begin writing with: Carpets rolled up . . .

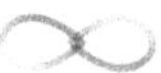

Day Sixteen
Select Calming Strategy One or Two

Creative Writing Setup Sixteen

September days brought a welcome relief from the heat, and the kids went back to school. In the stillness of the lunch hour, untying the strings, she reread his letters as though the writer was there with her. Pausing, she then wrote back, writing as though he sat there with her.

Creative Writing Starter Sixteen

Begin writing with: Gardening gloves on . . .

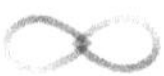

Day Seventeen
Select Calming Strategy One or Two

Creative Writing Setup Seventeen

The salty ocean spray on her face calmed her nerves and eased her nausea. The ship was filled with couples and families on their way to a new life. *If only she could feel the ground again*, she thought. She closed her eyes and thought of home.

Creative Writing Starter Seventeen

Begin writing with: Shoes needed to be polished . . .

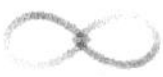

Day Eighteen
Select Calming Strategy One or Two

Creative Writing Setup Eighteen

Bringing the day's produce out onto the tables under the awning was the best part of his day. As the neighbors hurried by, he said a quick hello or waved his hand to each one. Sending others along with a smile was like sending his beloved children off to school.

Creative Writing Starter Eighteen

Begin writing with: Fumbling for the keys . . .

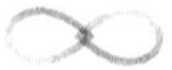

Day Nineteen
Select Calming Strategy One or Two

Creative Writing Setup Nineteen

After the shaking, pieces and shards of fine pottery spread out over the marble floor like stars sparkling in the deep night's sky. Disturbing nothing, they took photos, hoping to put everything back together again.

Creative Writing Starter Nineteen

Begin writing with: Feeling for the . . .

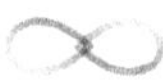

Day Twenty
Select Calming Strategy One or Two

Creative Writing Setup Twenty

Tossing his sweater on the table in silence, he turned and left the room. He did not see the sweater slip behind the table to the floor. In a hurry to go out again, irritated, he left without it.

Creative Writing Starter Twenty

Begin writing with: Porch lights . . .

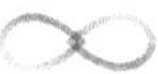

Day Twenty-One
Select Calming Strategy One or Two

Creative Writing Setup Twenty-One

Hissing, followed by a wailing like a baby's cry, broke the silence and sent me racing toward the commotion. Two cats faced off, neither one backing down. Grabbing the hose, I turned it on them full blast. They bolted in unison and disappeared in opposite directions.

Creative Writing Starter Twenty-One

Begin writing with: White cotton . . .

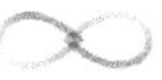

Day Twenty-Two
Select Calming Strategy One or Two

Creative Writing Setup Twenty-Two

"Hey, I decided what color to paint my house! No, actually, it says right here that the association decides," she muttered.

Silence followed as she read the rest of the agreement. As she returned to her home, visions of pink, purple, neon green, and orange danced in her head.

Creative Writing Starter Twenty-Two

Begin writing with: The dog-eared cookbook . . .

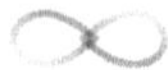

Day Twenty-Three
Select Calming Strategy One or Two

Creative Writing Setup Twenty-Three

Almost ready for the masquerade ball, they inspected the lines and seams of their costumes. Each pulled their hoods over their heads and tucked them into their collars. They were ready. No one would suspect who they really were— until it was time.

Creative Writing Starter Twenty-Three

Begin writing with: Taxis lined the curb . . .

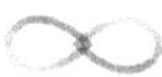

Day Twenty-Four
Select Calming Strategy One or Two

Creative Writing Setup Twenty-Four

Jumping up from their beds, jarred from sleep as the shrill sound of a fire alarm broke the silence, they found smoke wafting out the open doorway across the hall. The neighbors emerged, embarrassed and apologetic. They had burned their toast again.

Creative Writing Starter Twenty-Four

Begin writing with: Parcels piled up . . .

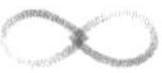

Day Twenty-Five
Select Calming Strategy One or Two

Creative Writing Setup Twenty-Five

Trailer trucks lined the road leading to the diner. Hungry and tired, the kids in the backseat dozed as the family car pulled into the little parking lot. Each parent carried a child. The father tugged the diner doors open. Bright lights, home cooking, and loud conversation instantly revived them.

Creative Writing Starter Twenty-Five

Begin writing with: Holding the porch swing . . .

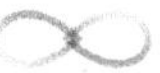

Day Twenty-Six
Select Calming Strategy One or Two

Creative Writing Setup Twenty-Six

Power outages happened often, so she had grown accustomed to lighting the candles now scattered about her apartment. Meals were always of the quick and easy variety. Tonight she sat in the dark, eating warmed soup and crackers, watching the stars put on their show.

Creative Writing Starter Twenty-Six

Begin writing with: Picking up the wet towels . . .

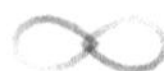

Day Twenty-Seven
Select Calming Strategy One or Two

Creative Writing Setup Twenty-Seven

Shadows of chairs grow longer and travel across the polished floor. Time-lapse photography records the shadow's silent daily journey from its appearance through its demise as the sun drops from the horizon. One change, small or large, will decide how, or if, that shadow returns the next day.

Creative Writing Starter Twenty-Seven

Begin writing with: Lavender and roses . . .

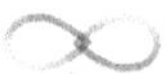

Day Twenty-Eight
Select Calming Strategy One or Two

Creative Writing Setup Twenty-Eight

Shoes and sandals filled the entryway, and a mountain of backpacks and suitcases spilled into the living room. The kitchen was a flurry of excitement as kids emptied the refrigerator into their beach bags. Summer had arrived!

Creative Writing Starter Twenty-Eight

Begin writing with: Baskets carried like . . .

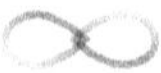

Day Twenty-Nine
Select Calming Strategy One or Two

Creative Writing Setup Twenty-Nine

She relaxed into the rhythm of the rain as it struck the windowpane and overflowed from the roof gutters onto roses and river stones below. Picking up the tempo, the north wind added an inconsistent thud as the swing struck the porch railing. A thunderous rumbling and wild crack of lightning split the oak tree open—her reverie was instantly over.

Creative Writing Starter Twenty-Nine

Begin writing with: Gloves lay on . . .

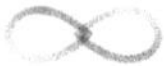

Day Thirty
Select Calming Strategy One or Two

Creative Writing Setup Thirty

Wildflower seeds had been a welcome treat for the birds. The squirrels had been busy moving the crocus bulbs around. Looking forward to Spring's garden, she scattered another bag of seeds.

Creative Writing Starter Thirty

Begin writing with: Stepping around . . .

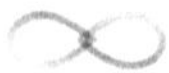

Day Thirty-One
Select Calming Strategy Three or Four

Creative Writing Setup Thirty-One

A crisp linen envelope slipped from the "to-do" file. In it, was a slim key tied on a card by a thin red ribbon. "For your next move" it said on one side, "cash box" on the other. Taking the box from the shelf, she could feel it was no longer empty.

Creative Writing Starter Thirty-One

Begin writing with: Sitting on the back steps . . .

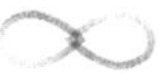

Day Thirty-Two
Select Calming Strategy Three or Four

Creative Writing Setup Thirty-Two

The fire crackled, and sparks flew up and out into the night. They huddled together just out of reach from the sparks that sometimes popped sideways. The hot sand was now cold, and the tide swept in, one wave at a time. Soon they would leave for home, carrying smoky clothes, clinging sand, and memories with which to sleep.

Creative Writing Starter Thirty-Two

Begin writing with: Cars slowed as . . .

Day Thirty-Three
Select Calming Strategy Three or Four

Creative Writing Setup Thirty-Three

Without a word, with fishing poles, bait, and food for the day onboard, they pushed the canoe out into the shallows and climbed in. The commotion disturbed the water and startled the nesting birds. Dipping their oars into the water, they coasted a moment as the lake accepted their presence. In an instant the silence returned. With a nod from the man at the stern, both paddles dug deeper and swept the boat through the stillness.

Creative Writing Starter Thirty-Three

Begin writing with: Seen in the distance . . .

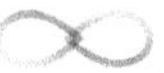

Day Thirty-Four
Select Calming Strategy Three or Four

Creative Writing Setup Thirty-Four

Every morning, the alarm would go off. She'd get up, toilet, wash her hands, brush the night from her mouth, and comb her hair. Then she'd pour instant coffee and butter toasted bread as she sat at her kitchen table and watched the light filter through windows and warm the floor. Nothing warmed her heart. Today, she awoke to coffee brewing, fresh cinnamon rolls baking, and bacon frying.

Creative Writing Starter Thirty-Four

Begin writing with: Feeling for the . . .

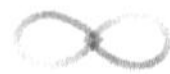

Day Thirty-Five
Select Calming Strategy Three or Four

Creative Writing Setup Thirty-Five

No one could sit for long on the hard benches in the park. The benches puzzled her because everything else about the place welcomed contemplation. The windows of the homes across from the park were covered and dark. The windows puzzled her because everything else about the homes welcomed visitors. People did not rest for long on a bench. Not many visitors came to the homes. Perhaps, she mused, that was the point.

Creative Writing Starter Thirty-Five

Begin writing with: Fingers on the keys . . .

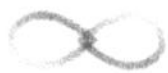

Day Thirty-Six
Select Calming Strategy Three or Four

Creative Writing Setup Thirty-Six

Whatever he could reach in the refrigerator he had lined up on the little table in front of him. Picking up the ketchup in one hand and the mustard in the other, he began squirting them in unison into a bowl in front of him.

"What are you doing?"

With great seriousness, he looked up and said, "A science project."

Creative Writing Starter Thirty-Six

Begin writing with: Two glasses of . . .

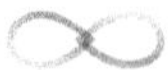

Day Thirty-Seven
Select Calming Strategy Three or Four

Creative Writing Setup Thirty-Seven

Fully outfitted for the game, as the big kids were, the little ones followed the black and white ball around the field like bees buzzing 'round their moving hive. That is, of course, supposing they would be knocking their hive about with nudges and blocks. Funniest of all were the parents on the sidelines.

Creative Writing Starter Thirty-Seven

Begin writing with: Tugging at the loose . . .

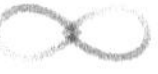

Day Thirty-Eight
Select Calming Strategy Three or Four

Creative Writing Setup Thirty-Eight

From the wings behind the curtain, he scanned the small group in the balcony, second row. They were those who would tell him the truth about the performance. He learned not by watching the performance or listening to the critics, it was always those in the balcony second row, he paid attention to.

Creative Writing Starter Thirty-Eight

Begin writing with: Emptying the last . . .

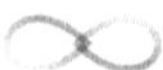

Day Thirty-Nine
Select Calming Strategy Three or Four

Creative Writing Setup Thirty-Nine

Fanning the pages and then pressing them gently open at intervals, the book would soon tell the story held within. Before long, the evening would fall quiet, and then when everyone else slept, the journey would begin.

Creative Writing Starter Thirty-Nine

Begin writing with: On the train from . . .

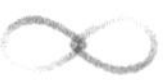

Day Forty
Select Calming Strategy Three or Four

Creative Writing Setup Forty

Finding herself transported into a small upper room carried her back in time. On the night's breeze, she moved around the Italian Master, as he brought the woman out of the canvas with his paint and his brush. He turned, his eyes met hers, and she suddenly became the woman on the canvas. Back in her room now, unknown minutes or hours later, she left, knowing what he needed her to know.

Creative Writing Starter Forty

Begin writing with: Footsteps above, quick and heavy . . .

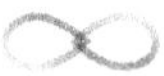

Day Forty-One
Select Calming Strategy Three or Four

Creative Writing Setup Forty-One

Mechanically reaching for the laundry detergent, she tried to recall how she got there. She was on autopilot again. Pushing the cart forward, she leaned over and put the detergent in the cart. She went in the direction of the floral department; some fresh flowers would inspire her as she put the groceries away.

Creative Writing Starter Forty-One

Begin writing with: Hummingbirds enjoyed . . .

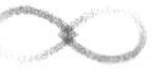

Day Forty-Two
Select Calming Strategy Three or Four

Creative Writing Setup Forty-Two

"Oh, you do make things complicated."
The voice of her grandmother's chiding rang clearly in her ears. It was as though she was right there with her. The memory of her smile was followed by the memory of her voice: "Let's go see if the library has any new books for us today." The strands of thoughts unwound themselves as she got in the car to go to the library.

Creative Writing Starter Forty-Two

Begin writing with: Wicker chairs . . .

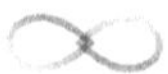

Day Forty-Three
Select Calming Strategy Three or Four

Creative Writing Setup Forty-Three

I watched as the afternoon rain fell down the shop window, making your reflection and the cakes on display inside dance together. The Baker's cat stepped lightly over your boots and dried her tail on your pant legs. Windows on the apartments above the shops were closed quickly as the bus stopped to pick up a young mother and her child. You stepped into the bakery to the welcome sound of bells.

Creative Writing Starter Forty-Three

Begin writing with: Large lines and larger . . .

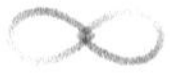

Day Forty-Four
Select Calming Strategy Three or Four

Creative Writing Setup Forty-Four

Except for litter, books, sweaters and lunch boxes left behind by the students, the halls of the school stood empty. A single figure moved slowly through the halls, sweeping, stooping, lifting and wiping. This was the time of year the caretaker loved best because he could now sing as loud and as long as he pleased.

Creative Writing Starter Forty-Four

Begin writing with: From behind the closed . . .

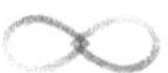

Day Forty-Five
Select Calming Strategy Three or Four

Creative Writing Setup Forty-Five

She woke to the rhythmic sounds of the travelers as they rushed past with right feet firmly working their gas pedals. Rising, she opened the window to take in the morning. The baker across the street waved hello as he swept the sidewalk. The sun cresting the cathedral in the distance reminded her of her childhood home. She loosened the belt on her dressing gown and turned to take her morning bath.

Creative Writing Starter Forty-Five

Begin writing with: Steamboats eased . . .

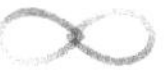

Day Forty-Six
Select Calming Strategy Three or Four

Creative Writing Setup Forty-Six

Last night's snowfall cast a silence that wrapped her heart in a mantle that inspired her as she wrote her letters. Sunlight streamed through the window, warming her paper. She found a flower stamp to put on the letter to her sister.

Creative Writing Starter Forty-Six

Begin writing with: Glasses laid . . .

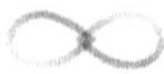

Day Forty-Seven
Select Calming Strategy Three or Four

Creative Writing Setup Forty-Seven

Screeching brakes and blaring horns broke through the sounds of the television. Sitting still, they listened for ensuing crashing, crunching of metal, shouting and sirens. None came. The usual hum of traffic continued. Their attention went back to the television, to rewinding the show to before the interruption.

Creative Writing Starter Forty-Seven

Begin writing with: Chairs lined the walls . . .

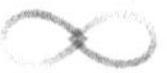

Day Forty-Eight
Select Calming Strategy Three or Four

Creative Writing Setup Forty-Eight

Her neighbor's dogs would alert them each time others came and went. No matter how quietly she moved, the dogs knew when she was outside her door. She found it comforting because it was as if they were saying goodbye and hello to her each day.

Creative Writing Starter Forty-Eight

Begin writing with: Flowering tomato plants . . .

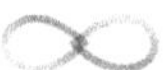

Day Forty-Nine
Select Calming Strategy Three or Four

Creative Writing Setup Forty-Nine

Yellowed, stained and tattered, the old woman's cookbook was now kept in a manila envelope. Even though she knew each recipe by heart, she would leaf through the pages until she found the one she would make that day. Going down the list of ingredients, she would find and place each one on the counter, then read and follow each step—just as her mother had taught her to do.

Creative Writing Starter Forty-Nine

Begin writing with: Touching the tabletop . . .

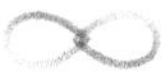

Day Fifty
Select Calming Strategy Three or Four

Creative Writing Setup Fifty

Ice cream curled into the ice cream cone like a wave out of the ocean. Bending down to the tiny outstretched hands, the ice cream vendor smiled as the child held the treat as though holding a precious gift.

Creative Writing Starter Fifty

Begin writing with: Umbrellas were not . . .

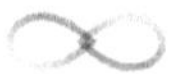

Day Fifty-One
Select Calming Strategy Three or Four

Creative Writing Setup Fifty-One

As far as she could see, there were only clouds and open sky. The plane had been below the clouds one minute, then through and above them the next. Breaking through the clouds was like breaking through the heaviness in her heart.

Creative Writing Starter Fifty-One

Begin writing with: Tape measure and . . .

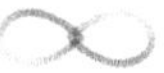

Day Fifty-Two
Select Calming Strategy Three or Four

Creative Writing Setup Fifty-Two

Skateboarders lined the park's ramp, waiting for the competition to begin. Anticipation grew as each contestant's practice session timed out and the next skateboarder rolled onto the ramp. Finally, cheers erupted as the sportscaster began the competition.

Creative Writing Starter Fifty-Two

Begin writing with: Through a hole . . .

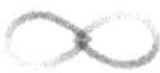

Day Fifty-Three
Select Calming Strategy Three or Four

Creative Writing Setup Fifty-Three

Two sneakers, one right, one left, toes stuffed with paper, laces braided and nestled together in the just-big-enough box . . . waited. They wondered who would buy them, what adventures would they go on. One rainy day, their box was opened, and they were put on a little boy. They were all smiles and chattering as the boy lifted his toes and banged his heels on the floor. They were on their way! Out the door they went, into a deep puddle. What an adventure they were on!

Creative Writing Starter Fifty-Three

Begin writing with: Beside the open . . .

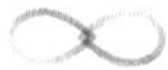

Day Fifty-Four
Select Calming Strategy Three or Four

Creative Writing Setup Fifty-Four

A last-minute call and she was finally on her way! So far everything was working like clockwork. Then came a red light. No problem, a minute or so; no worries. A woman walking, meandering really, caught her eye. There was something familiar about her, she wasn't sure what, but her movements held her attention. Slowly the woman raised her head and their eyes met. A car's horn blared behind her. The light was now green. She went through the light and parked her car. She got out, only to find the woman was gone. The moment, like the red light had passed.

Creative Writing Starter Fifty-Four

Begin writing with: Blankets folded . . .

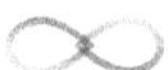

Day Fifty-Five
Select Calming Strategy Three or Four

Creative Writing Setup Fifty-Five

Nothing moved outside, not even the mosquitos. Humidity hung in the air, draping the bicycles, swings and grass. Nothing moved inside, not even the children. The window air conditioner labored slowly, making no difference in the temperature in the room. They hoped the clouds would break soon and clear the air.

Creative Writing Starter Fifty-Five

Begin writing with: Springs poked through . . .

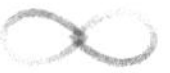

Day Fifty-Six
Select Calming Strategy Three or Four

Creative Writing Setup Fifty-Six

Looking first at the plastic-covered photo in front of her, she then looked at the driver's face reflected back to her from the rearview mirror. The driver was much older than the photo: hair had thinned and greyed, his face had been weathered by the nights of driving and days of working construction. It was him though. The smile in his eyes and at the corners of his mouth would help her recognize him no matter where she found him or how old he'd grown.

Creative Writing Starter Fifty-Six

Begin writing with: Green bottles of . . .

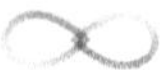

Day Fifty-Seven
Select Calming Strategy Three or Four

Creative Writing Setup Fifty-Seven

Soot darkened the paint on the ceiling above the old candle sconce. She had always known when he was home because the room would go dark when he opened the door. She no longer lit the candle because the years had taken him from her. Yet the soot remained, and she remembered his coming home.

Creative Writing Starter Fifty-Seven

Begin writing with: Listening to the rumbling . . .

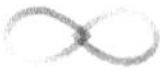

Day Fifty-Eight
Select Calming Strategy Three or Four

Creative Writing Setup Fifty-Eight

Heavy metal chairs being pulled across the concrete and stone patio grated on her nerves. She put on her headphones and tuned into the heavy-metal music station. This sound soothed her nerves.

Creative Writing Starter Fifty-Eight

Begin writing with: Another toothbrush and . . .

Day Fifty-Nine
Select Calming Strategy Three or Four

Creative Writing Setup Fifty-Nine

The family of squirrels loved it when the new family of humans moved in. In winter, their porch always had an ample supply of the sweetest seeds and the humans were always glad to see them, especially the little girl. They had fun watching her as she tried to talk to them.

Creative Writing Starter Fifty-Nine

Begin writing with: Three steps away . . .

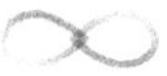

Day Sixty
Select Calming Strategy Three or Four

Creative Writing Setup Sixty

Laughter filled the backyard as the children splashed about in the kiddie's pool in their raincoats, rain boots and umbrellas under the noonday sun. As the sprinkler rotated around, the pitch of joy rose so high that even the old retriever lying behind the patio door woke up and barked to be let out to join the children.

Creative Writing Starter Sixty

Begin writing with: Whispering so as to not . . .

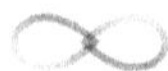

Day Sixty-One
Select Calming Strategy Five or Six

Creative Writing Setup Sixty-One

Almost every crumb of the cake was gone. Now what was she supposed to do? No one was home, yet it was *gone*. Reaching into the cupboard for a box of cake mix, she hoped there was enough time to bake another.

Creative Writing Starter Sixty-One

Begin writing with: Floodlights gave . . .

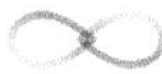

Day Sixty-Two
Select Calming Strategy Five or Six

Creative Writing Setup Sixty-Two

They wondered, as they sat perched at the tips of the branches, what the humans were doing. Rain or shine, every day, all day, they walked, rode buggies and whacked little round balls up and down between the trees. They found it amusing when the balls disappeared below the trees because the humans would move about in the most hilarious motions.

Creative Writing Starter Sixty-Two

Begin writing with: Water stains on . . .

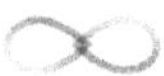

Day Sixty-Three
Select Calming Strategy Five or Six

Creative Writing Setup Sixty-Three

"Raining cats and dogs", what a silly thing to say, but he would say it every time it rained—whether it was a heavy rain or not. Rainy days were one of their favorite times. She stood behind the big window, looking at a real "raining cats and dogs" rain. She smiled, pulled on her rain boots, wrapped her sweater about her and, picking up his umbrella, opened the door and stepped out into the downpour.

Creative Writing Starter Sixty-Three

Begin writing with: Power to the toaster . . .

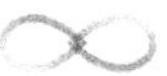

Day Sixty-Four
Select Calming Strategy Five or Six

Creative Writing Setup Sixty-Four

The plane rolled up and she waved from the gate. No matter that she could not see them, she waved in case they were looking from their seats and could see her. With her picture identification in hand she waited patiently. It was lunchtime and she knew just where she'd suggest they stop for lunch.

Creative Writing Starter Sixty-Four

Begin writing with: Tying the knot . . .

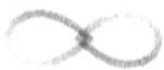

Day Sixty-Five
Select Calming Strategy Five or Six

Creative Writing Setup Sixty-Five

As she rubbed the silver polish onto the vase, she never ceased to marvel at how quickly the silver became clean and shiny. Carrying the vase to the shed she could see her reflection clearly, as if in a mirror. The gardener came in with an armful of roses for the vase. In no time, the vase and roses were on the table in the entryway, greeting everyone with their brilliance and sweet aroma.

Creative Writing Starter Sixty-Five

Begin writing with: Signs covered in . . .

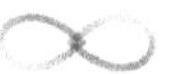

Day Sixty-Six
Select Calming Strategy Five or Six

Creative Writing Setup Sixty-Six

Right, left, right left. The children marched up and down the street, arm in arm, for no particular reason. They told the onlookers, "Just for something to do." Soon they began exaggerating their steps and it looked like they were sweeping the street with their feet. The whole scene drew laughter from the neighbors. Soon everyone was joining hands together and parading up and down the street with them.

Creative Writing Starter Sixty-Six

Begin writing with: Important times are . . .

Day Sixty-Seven
Select Calming Strategy Five or Six

Creative Writing Setup Sixty-Seven

Drip, drip, drip. Water drops falling from the spout onto the dishes in the sink soon made a small pool. They'd been gone for a week and the water level rose to overflowing and, one drip at a time, fell on the floor. Upon their return the water had reached the back door.

Creative Writing Starter Sixty-Seven

Begin writing with: Red, white and blue . . .

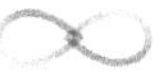

Day Sixty-Eight
Select Calming Strategy Five or Six

Creative Writing Setup Sixty-Eight

Springtime brought new buds, new promise, on trees outside her window. These trees had become her friends and she enjoyed seeing them come to life after the long winter.

Creative Writing Starter Sixty-Eight

Begin writing with: Digging great big . . .

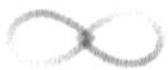

Day Sixty-Nine
Select Calming Strategy Five or Six

Creative Writing Setup Sixty-Nine

She pulled off the bow and tore open the wrapping paper. Into her lap fell crayons and coloring books and two sketchbooks. This was not just any box of crayons, but a great big box of 152 colors! Looking outside at the gray rainy day, then back to her new box of crayons she suddenly felt just a little bit better.

Creative Writing Starter Sixty-Nine

Begin writing with: Turning over . . .

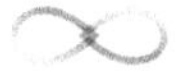

Day Seventy
Select Calming Strategy Five or Six

Creative Writing Setup Seventy

The blackness of the night sky was nearly complete. Thick clouds cast a shroud over the moon. Gravel crunched under our boots and it felt as if we were the only two humans in miles. A feeling of freedom surrounded us. Only the sounds of our breath and steps could be heard. These rhythms kept our focus centered in the now.

Creative Writing Starter Seventy

Begin writing with: A hint of lavender . . .

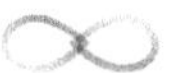

Day Seventy-One

Select Calming Strategy Five or Six

Creative Writing Setup Seventy-One

Audience laughter bordered on hysteria. Surprisingly, it was infectious. Stage lights were bright; the actors exaggerated. Never mind the shoddy curtain and crud between the floorboards—spectators were transported to where mystery was commonplace. It was a disruption from current reality and a short-term panacea for those who needed an escape.

Creative Writing Starter Seventy-One

Begin writing with: Icy roads . . .

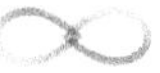

Day Seventy-Two

Select Calming Strategy Five or Six

Creative Writing Setup Seventy-Two

The smell of old books brought a sneeze to her nose. Dust and leather, mixed with mildew, created an almost overpowering odor. The room was pleasant only because of the tomes standing at attention on ancient oak shelves. Because the door remained ajar, the smell began to dissipate. Soon the fragrance disappeared, enticing her to pull up an armchair, stoke the non-existent fire and rest amidst her favorite friends.

Creative Writing Starter Seventy-Two

Begin writing with: Intense light infused . . .

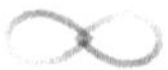

Day Seventy-Three
Select Calming Strategy Five or Six

Creative Writing Setup Seventy-Three

She rested comfortably leaning over the old wooden fence. The sun beat down on her back and she let its rays massage away the strain and stress that had accompanied her here. She had become bone-weary, but warmth from the mid-afternoon sun brought life to her soul. She lifted her chin and her hat fell back into the dirt. She let the sun caress her exhausted being, allowing its energy to rejuvenate and restore.

Creative Writing Starter **Seventy-Three**

Begin writing with: The taste was exotic . . .

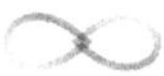

Day Seventy-Four
Select Calming Strategy Five or Six

Creative Writing Setup Seventy-Four

The fresh-from-the-orchard peaches oozed through his fingers and dripped down his cleft chin. His bright blue eyes sparkled with delight. His pudgy hands continued to squish the delicious fruit, letting little rivers of juice spill down his arms until he was a sticky, sopping wet mess of peach and exuberant joy.

Creative Writing Starter Seventy-Four

Begin writing with: Patiently they walked down the narrow corridor . . .

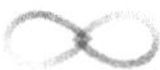

Day Seventy-Five
Select Calming Strategy Five or Six

Creative Writing Setup Seventy-Five

Soft, lilac-colored curtains danced as the cool spring breeze roused her from her nap. The air was drenched with rain, the temperature chilly to her skin. She stretched like a cat, yawning and extending her bare arms as freshness tickled her body and wind toyed with her tousled hair.

Creative Writing Starter Seventy-Five

Begin writing with: The parking lot was jammed with . . .

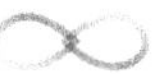

Day Seventy-Six
Select Calming Strategy Five or Six

Creative Writing Setup Seventy-Six

Chipped china and piecemeal silver graced the rough-hewn tables. The crowd was thin this morning, but it wouldn't take long and people would arrive in droves. Pulled-pork and savory beans were bubbling happily in gigantic electric roasters. The aroma of home-baked cornbread aroused olfactory senses. Children were chasing and jumping and laughing. Adults were unhurriedly setting up, preparing for a leisurely day of sun and sweat and food and fellowship.

Creative Writing Starter Seventy-Six

Begin writing with: Gently she carried her bundle toward . . .

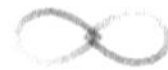

Day Seventy-Seven
Select Calming Strategy Five or Six

Creative Writing Setup Seventy-Seven

The sauna reached its therapeutic temperature. Sweat dripped down cheeks and heads lolled against wooden walls. Mist created an ethereal plane where each sat in their own little world, drained from hotness and resting in a place of separation. Cedar-scent permeated the small room; conversations stalled as bodies relaxed in heat's grip.

Creative Writing Starter Seventy-Seven

Begin writing with: Elbows jutted and knees bent . . .

Day Seventy-Eight
Select Calming Strategy Five or Six

Creative Writing Setup Seventy-Eight

Traffic was fierce. Horns blasted and exhaust billowed from far too many vehicles in the commerce-infested locale. Pedestrians walked with heads lowered, robotically scrolling, tapping, and swiping at their devices. Near-casualties abounded. Each was an island unto themself, stoically marching onward.

Creative Writing Starter Seventy-Eight

Begin writing with: Toes wiggled in the frigid water while laughter erupted . . .

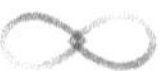

Day Seventy-Nine
Select Calming Strategy Five or Six

Creative Writing Setup Seventy-Nine

The dessert was delectable—a soft creamy center amidst a deep chocolate shell. Coffee was poured while the jovial host entertained with news of his travels. Hope was restored as his story unraveled, giving answers to worries and context to confusion. The guests leaned back, satisfied with the cuisine and the narrative, both stirring expectation and optimism.

Creative Writing Starter Seventy-Nine

Begin writing with: Hiking up a steep incline . . .

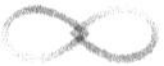

Day Eighty
Select Calming Strategy Five or Six

Creative Writing Setup Eighty

The cacophony of languages assaulted her ears. She reveled in the chaos. Smiles and frowns, angry gestures and nurturing postures filled the dirt-packed street. She was never more alive than when she was following her passion, her dreams, and her vision. She lived for these days, rescuing those who could not rescue themselves.

Creative Writing Starter Eighty

Begin writing with: Rain pelted the metal roof, drumming . . .

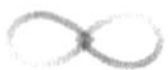

Day Eighty-One
Select Calming Strategy Five or Six

Creative Writing Setup Eighty-One

Small hands and twinkling eyes gazed out onto the street as she parted the blinds. She was looking for someone, someone who was not likely to let her down. My chest tightened at the pent-up anticipation radiating off the small body. She giggled. Her special someone had arrived and there was nothing left to do but race from the window and dive into his protective arms.

Creative Writing Starter Eighty-One

Begin writing with: Crickets chirped their night song . . .

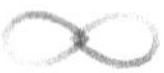

Day Eighty-Two
Select Calming Strategy Five or Six

Creative Writing Setup Eighty-Two

She stared at the marble floor while the incessant rhythm of the escalator and the vibration of the steel structure around her quieted her mind and numbed her feelings. Turning her wrist over again, her eyes went from the face of the watch to the faces of the passersby.

Creative Writing Starter Eighty-Two

Begin writing with: Buttoning his vest . . .

Day Eighty-Three
Select Calming Strategy Five or Six

Creative Writing Setup Eighty-Three

Out of the line of trees stepped the most magnificent creature they had ever seen. Stopping in their tracks, they held their breath and stood like statues. The deer raised her nose in the air as she turned her head to look at them. One ear twitched, then her weight shifted and she turned, her legs leaping up and forward in one powerful motion. In an instant she was gone, gone into the safety of the deep woods. They remained standing there a long time.

Creative Writing Starter Eighty-Three

Begin writing with: Buttoning his vest . . .

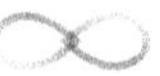

Day Eighty-Four
Select Calming Strategy Five or Six

Creative Writing Setup Eighty-Four

After piling the trunk of the car full to overflowing with their suitcases, duffle bags and backpacks, they stood there in silence. The night air was as thick as the darkness. Looking about for a hint of morning light, he closed the trunk with a heavy hand. The noise split the silence open.

Creative Writing Starter Eighty-Four

Begin writing with: Between the cotton . . .

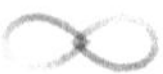

Day Eighty-Five
Select Calming Strategy Five or Six

Creative Writing Setup Eighty-Five

Once, concrete had poured into the earth for days on end, deeper than the tower would rise. The building constructed here would stand for almost a generation as the tallest building in the world. She preferred to look up, with her feet firmly planted on the ground, to enjoy the view. For a view from the top she chose to enjoy photos others had taken from their own journeys.

Creative Writing Starter Eighty-Five

Begin writing with: Beach Balls and . . .

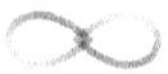

Day Eighty-Six
Select Calming Strategy Five or Six

Creative Writing Setup Eighty-Six

Sewing machines whirred along while yards and yards of satin and lace passed between the pressure foot and feed dog. Spools and bobbins of thread emptied as the seamstress created the dress that would be worn by the Queen at her marriage. There were months to go but no time to waste.

Creative Writing Starter Eighty-Six

Begin writing with: Bicycles on cobblestone . . .

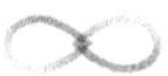

Day Eighty-Seven
Select Calming Strategy Five or Six
Creative Writing Setup Eighty-Seven

She stood before the mirror with her mother's dress, sweater and high-heeled shoes on. She spun and swayed back and forth, watching her body as she pretended to dance. Something was missing. Ah, yes, earrings and lipstick! Now she was all grown up, even if just for a few minutes.

Creative Writing Starter Eighty-Seven

Begin writing with: White lilies . . .

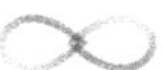

Day Eighty-Eight
Select Calming Strategy Five or Six

Creative Writing Setup Eighty-Eight

Time to go. Pulling the rose-print dress from the closet, she slipped it on over her head. She checked her bag for keys, phone, wallet and lipstick. She was ready. She waited in anticipation by the kitchen door.

Creative Writing Starter Eighty-Eight

Begin writing with: Old bricks cast . . .

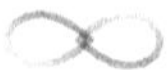

Day Eighty-Nine
Select Calming Strategy Five or Six

Creative Writing Setup Eighty-Nine

At the end of the lane, past the stand of trees, sat a little cottage made of stone wall. Coarse wooden window boxes hung beneath the windows of the house. Deep red geraniums spilled out of the boxes and down to the lavender and rose bushes below.

Creative Writing Starter Eighty-Nine

Begin writing with: Scissors sharpened for . . .

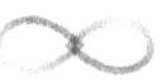

Day Ninety
Select Calming Strategy Five or Six

Creative Writing Setup Ninety

Dandelions bloomed across the lawn, creating a striking carpet of yellow in a neighborhood of finely-trimmed green lawns.

"Why don't they spray and get rid of the dandelions?" his daughter asked.

"I suppose it's because they like them," her father replied with a hint of a chuckle in his words.

Creative Writing Starter Ninety

Begin writing with: Always is such a . . .

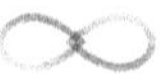

Day Ninety-One
Select Calming Strategy Seven or Eight

Creative Writing Setup Ninety-One

Sleeping bags and pillows covered the living room floor. The house was buzzing with the activity only teenagers on summer vacation could create. She looked at her watch and knew they would be off to the beach shortly. Standing still, she closed her eyes, listened and smiled. She would remember this for a long time.

Creative Writing Starter Ninety-One

Begin writing with: Lifting the cake from the . . .

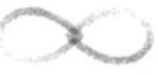

Day Ninety-Two
Select Calming Strategy Seven or Eight

Creative Writing Setup Ninety-Two

She could turn and close off the world by turning off her phone, TV, and computer, drawing the blinds and pulling the covers over her head. But she could not silence the past that wound its way even into her unconscious as she slept. One day, a hummingbird drew her outside into the sunshine and its world.

Creative Writing Starter Ninety-Two

Begin writing with: Between the cotton . . .

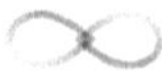

Day Ninety-Three
Select Calming Strategy Seven or Eight

Creative Writing Setup Ninety-Three

Hurrying along the dry dirt path, the boys kicked a loose stone along between them as if it was a soccer ball. They exaggerate their movements, enjoying every imagined goal and the resulting cheers.

Creative Writing Starter Ninety-Three

Begin writing with: Willow tree branches draped . . .

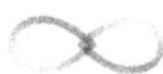

Day Ninety-Four
Select Calming Strategy Seven or Eight

Creative Writing Setup Ninety-Four

He stepped out into the bitter cold morning, where even his breath froze on the scarf wrapped round his face and neck. Pulling an imaginary extra layer around him, curling his shoulders up to his ears and dropping his chin to his chest, he squinted to focus on the field before him.

Creative Writing Starter Ninety-Four

Begin writing with: Keys and gloves . . .

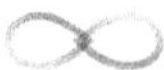

Day Ninety-Five
Select Calming Strategy Seven or Eight

Creative Writing Setup Ninety-Five

An abrupt awakening, from a deep sleep, confused and irritated her. What had jarred her out of her deep sleep? She only heard the sound of the waves lapping against the shore and the dull thud of the boat as it brushed up against the bumpers on the side of the dock.

Creative Writing Starter Ninety-Five

Begin writing with: Laughter erupted from . . .

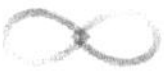

Day Ninety-Six
Select Calming Strategy Seven or Eight

Creative Writing Setup Ninety-Six

Out from between the warm blankets she slides into the crisp pre-dawn day. Trees remain hidden by the darkness. She resists turning on the lamp. Instead, she enjoys exploring her world in its darkness as it waits to be painted by the rising sun.

Creative Writing Starter Ninety-Six

Begin writing with: Toys spilled out . . .

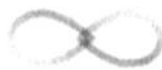

Day Ninety-Seven
Select Calming Strategy Seven or Eight

Creative Writing Setup Ninety-Seven

It had been twenty miles, at least, since she used the gas pedal. Well maybe not; maybe one mile. Still, she was frustrated and moving toward being irate. Looking around, she noticed other drivers. They were looking around, too, some of them singing along to some song; many were enjoying this time. She soon began to discover plants, buildings, signs, and the horizon that she had not noticed before.

Creative Writing Starter Ninety-Seven

Begin writing with: Wrapped in a blanket . . .

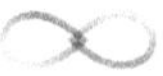

Day Ninety-Eight
Select Calming Strategy Seven or Eight

Creative Writing Setup Ninety-Eight

She stood at the ironing board and watched daytime T.V. until the heap of shirts on the couch on one side became pressed and hung neatly on the rack on the other side. She could not recall ironing the shirts, what shows or ads she had seen. Two hours had passed. She sighed as she hung the shirts in the closet and put the iron and board away.

Creative Writing Starter Ninety-Eight

Begin writing with: As the tide came in . . .

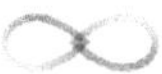

Day Ninety-Nine
Select Calming Strategy Seven or Eight

Creative Writing Setup Ninety-Nine

Out into the garden she went with her gloves, pruning shears and basket in hand. She smiled as she approached the rose bushes. Soon her basket was full, and the bushes hardly showed where she'd clipped. She loved this time of year when roses filled the garden and her home with their fragrance.

Creative Writing Starter Ninety-Nine

Begin writing with: Pink paint dripped . . .

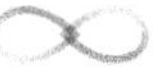

Day One-Hundred
Select Calming Strategy Seven or Eight

Creative Writing Setup One Hundred

"I know it's in here." Then he whispered, "It has to be here!" He had ignored the panic rising from his stomach, but now that it was in his throat he quickly sat down on the side of the bed. *Breathe and relax. Breathe and relax,* he told himself. Better. He turned his head and his eyes fell on the chest at the end of the bed. He opened the top and there it was.

Creative Writing Starter One Hundred

Begin writing with: Antique china teapots . . .

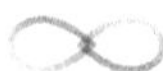

Day One-Hundred-One
Select Calming Strategy Seven or Eight

Creative Writing Setup One-Hundred-One

Every house looked the same. Even the blinds on the windows were the same. Only the numbers by the front door under the porch light were different. After parking her car in front of number 157, she looked in her things for the lace curtains and curtain rod. Before she did anything else, she would hang these in the kitchen window.

Creative Writing Starter One-Hundred-One

Begin writing with: Sand crabs and . . .

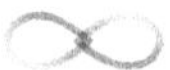

Day One-Hundred-Two
Select Calming Strategy Seven or Eight

Creative Writing Setup One-Hundred-Two

Years of dust lay thick on the covered furniture. The heavy brocade drapes hung in shreds, as though the dust had become so heavy in their fibers that gravity broke the cross-weave fibers as it pulled the dust to the ground. Standing in the doorway she whispered to the empty room, "Where shall we start?"

Creative Writing Starter One-Hundred-Two

Begin writing with: Lining the hallway walls . . .

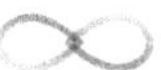

Day One-Hundred-Three
Select Calming Strategy Seven or Eight

Creative Writing Setup One-Hundred-Three

People filed off and onto the trains as they came and went. She often felt their movements looked like bugs. She joined the others on her platform.

Creative Writing Starter One-Hundred-Three

Begin writing with: Computer screens lit up . . .

Day One-Hundred-Four
Select Calming Strategy Seven or Eight

Creative Writing Setup One-Hundred-Four

Sally suggested, "Just step out at lunch and go in any direction. Go for five minutes, turn around, and come back."

She snapped, "Five and five make ten! Who has ten minutes any time of the day to do that!"

Sally was silent as she let the words hang in the air.

Creative Writing Starter One-Hundred-Four

Begin writing with: Colored pencils lay broken . . .

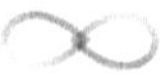

Day One-Hundred-Five
Select Calming Strategy Seven or Eight

Creative Writing Setup One-Hundred-Five

"Now just how do I get this thing to work?" she said under her breath while pushing buttons.

"Need some assistance?"

She looked over her glasses and saw the new computer guy with that genuine smile of his.

"Yes, thank you," she answered, because he had not used the word "help."

Creative Writing Starter One-Hundred-Five

Begin writing with: With a grocery cart full . . .

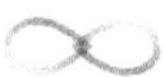

Day One-Hundred-Six
Select Calming Strategy Seven or Eight

Creative Writing Setup One-Hundred-Six

Boxes of files lined the room and their helpers kept bringing them in. The sisters looked in vain for labels or dates, a department; anything that would tell them what was in each box. Nothing. They would have to open each one. They hoped aloud that the contents in each box had not been mixed up as well. They opened the first few boxes: no such luck.

Creative Writing Starter One-Hundred-Six

Begin writing with: Summer breeze made . . .

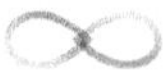

Day One-Hundred-Seven
Select Calming Strategy Seven or Eight

Creative Writing Setup One-Hundred-Seven

Salmon propelled themselves forward against the current, urged on by some unknown force to the place they would spawn. The children watched in amazement, wondering what was driving them. An old couple said they had come to watch this every year and they still could not explain it. They could only marvel.

Creative Writing Starter One-Hundred-Seven

Begin writing with: At the county fair . . .

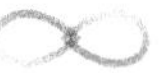

Day One-Hundred-Eight
Select Calming Strategy Seven or Eight

Creative Writing Setup One-Hundred-Eight

Swinging their legs over the wooden dock into the lake, they kicked and swirled their feet as the water splashed up over their summer outfits. The best part was that they would soon be scolded for getting everything wet. But they knew it would be okay—their clothes would soon dry and they would have had a lot of fun.

Creative Writing Starter One-Hundred-Eight

Begin writing with: Silver and gold . . .

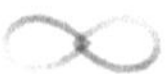

Day One-Hundred-Nine
Select Calming Strategy Seven or Eight

Creative Writing Setup One-Hundred-Nine

Tents lined the bank of the dry creek bed. The tents had appeared overnight. It was the first day of summer vacation. Coming over the hill, the children blinked when they saw their play place had been transformed into a place where homeless people lived.

Creative Writing Starter One-Hundred-Nine

Begin writing with: Dogs of all sizes . . .

Day One-Hundred-Ten
Select Calming Strategy Seven or Eight

Creative Writing Setup One-Hundred-Ten

Baggage claim, with its groaning and creaking carrousel and cavernous area had transformed into the greeting place where loved ones and business contacts met their arriving guests.

The walk from the gate helped to shake off the confinement of the airplane.

Creative Writing Starter One-Hundred-Ten

Begin writing with: Lifted into the cab . . .

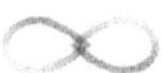

Day One-Hundred-Eleven
Select Calming Strategy Seven or Eight

Creative Writing Setup One-Hundred-Eleven

Peering up the full height of the building, she felt so small. Taking a deep breath and gripping her briefcase, she started for the door, growing bolder with each step.

Creative Writing Starter One-Hundred-Eleven

Begin writing with: Lunch boxes lined . . .

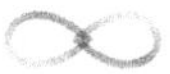

Day One-Hundred-Twelve
Select Calming Strategy Seven or Eight

Creative Writing Setup One-Hundred-Twelve

Her memory had faded. She ignored the whispers around her. What if she could not say what year it was, what kind of flowers she saw, or recite her address? Her heart knew and remembered without words what was most valuable. There was no reason to fret over the loss of details when her love of life remained.

Creative Writing Starter One-Hundred-Twelve

Begin writing with: Shadows grew long . . .

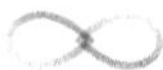

Day One-Hundred-Thirteen
Select Calming Strategy Seven or Eight

Creative Writing Setup One-Hundred-Thirteen

Out of the corner of her eye the coiled hose moved. She froze. The hose was over there. She slowly slid her backpack down her side, so it rested between her leg and the snake, then let the sleeve of her jacket drop to her wrist and pulled her hand up close to the inside of her sleeve. Three steps and she would be on the other side of the fence.

Creative Writing Starter One-Hundred-Thirteen

Begin writing with: Toasters and coffee makers . . .

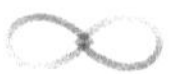

Day One-Hundred-Fourteen
Select Calming Strategy Seven or Eight

Creative Writing Setup One-Hundred-Fourteen

Sidewalks swelled with workers as office buildings emptied. The scene looked like a swift moving stream as a steady line of people dropped down into the caverns that held the underground trains, then emerged again onto quieter streets farther away. Personal lives opened as work lives closed their doors.

Creative Writing Starter One-Hundred-Fourteen

Begin writing with: Mud caked . . .

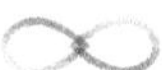

Day One-Hundred-Fifteen
Select Calming Strategy Seven or Eight

Creative Writing Setup One-Hundred-Fifteen

From her windows above the street she could see the world go by. There was more to see on the street than there was on the television. She would often join the throngs below and walk the streets, too. Coming home one day she looked up and saw a face in her window looking down at her.

Creative Writing Starter One-Hundred-Fifteen

Begin writing with: Umbrellas and raincoats . . .

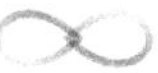

Day One-Hundred-Sixteen
Select Calming Strategy Seven or Eight

Creative Writing Setup One-Hundred-Sixteen

"Right then," he shouted. "Let's go." They followed him away from the baggage carousel and out the doors. Waving his hand wildly, he said, "Over here!"

A woman jumped from the van and greeted them. "Hello, hi everyone! Pile in kids!" The man tossed bags into the back, then jumped into the driver's seat, and with a quick look over his shoulder he pulled sharply out into traffic. Another ride pulled in right behind his van to act out the same abrupt greeting.

Creative Writing Starter One-Hundred-Sixteen

Begin writing with: Glass doors with . . .

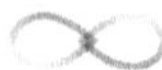

Day One-Hundred-Seventeen
Select Calming Strategy Seven or Eight

Creative Writing Setup One-Hundred-Seventeen

Behind the restaurant each night the old man played his violin. On his break the young man would watch and listen—feel really—the music the old man played. The young man would bring out a big piece of apple pie with ice cream to share, and two coffees. The old man would always say, "This is just like when I was a young man in the old country."

Creative Writing Starter One-Hundred-Seventeen

Begin writing with: Trucks rolled out . . .

Day One-Hundred-Eighteen
Select Calming Strategy Seven or Eight

Creative Writing Setup One-Hundred-Eighteen

Walking the long road north under the moonlit sky, they looked to the stars to guide them. Hiding during the light of day, they listened to the songs of the slaves in the fields to encourage them. She had been up and down this road many times, but she would never shake the fear, nor shed her hope.

Creative Writing Starter One-Hundred-Eighteen

Begin writing with: Brilliant colors . . .

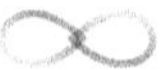

Day One-Hundred-Nineteen
Select Calming Strategy Seven or Eight

Creative Writing Setup One-Hundred-Nineteen

The table was ten feet long and filled with every kind of desert imaginable.

"I've got ten days, and this table is here all day and night," she mused. She figured she would sample the smallest of whatever she chose at each meal, and at snack time too. She began with a chocolate éclair.

Creative Writing Starter One-Hundred-Nineteen

Begin writing with: Dumping the bag . . .

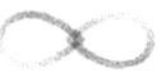

Day One-Hundred-Twenty
Select Calming Strategy Seven or Eight

Creative Writing Setup One-Hundred-Twenty

Cutting onions was no laughing matter. She avoided it whenever she could. She loved it when someone happened into the kitchen when she needed onions sliced or chopped. Everyone tried to remember to stay away when she was making dinner in case she needed them for that chore. That is, until one day, when one of them figured out how to cut the onion so it did not make them cry.

Creative Writing Starter One-Hundred-Twenty

Begin writing with: Pirate ships . . .

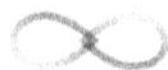

Day One-Hundred-Twenty-One
Select Calming Strategy Nine or Ten

Creative Writing Setup One-Hundred-Twenty-One

When she checked into the old motel by the lake, the desk clerk mentioned off-handedly, "The morning train comes through at four a.m. every day but Sunday." Then he gave her the keys to the cottage and pointed to his left. "Twenty-three is down there, on your right. Enjoy your stay."

She was roused from her slumber at 3:45 a.m. by a low rumbling that grew louder and began to shake the cottage and everything in it—including her. No sleeping in on this vacation!

Creative Writing Starter One-Hundred-Twenty-One

Begin writing with: Rocks lined . . .

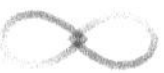

Day One-Hundred-Twenty-Two
Select Calming Strategy Nine or Ten

Creative Writing Setup One-Hundred-Twenty-Two

Grandpa took them into town in his motorboat. He would watch over the kids as he gave them turns driving the boat. Really, he thought, they were steering but they called it driving and he did not correct them. With their lifejackets on and holding tightly onto the boat, they bounced over the waves and enjoyed the fresh water spray on their faces.

Creative Writing Starter One-Hundred-Twenty-Two

Begin writing with: One pound of chocolate fudge . . .

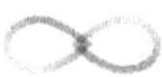

Day One-Hundred-Twenty-Three
Select Calming Strategy Nine or Ten

Creative Writing Setup One-Hundred-Twenty-Three

Her mother's ring weighed heavy on her finger. It was as if it was telling her, or she was telling it, that it did not belong to her. She had worn it long enough. Her fingers ran across it, like she had done so many times when her mother wore it. Letting the experiences go with a sigh, she took the ring off. She would give it to her niece. The ring didn't seem to want to belong to her.

Creative Writing Starter One-Hundred-Twenty-Three

Begin writing with: Pockets of salt . . .

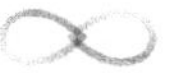

Day One-Hundred-Twenty-Five
Select Calming Strategy Nine or Ten

Creative Writing Setup One-Hundred-Twenty-Four

Their phones rang in unison; a knowing passed between their eyes.

"Something has happened. We need you here, both if possible, as soon as you can get here, safely of course."

She nodded and hung up.

The voice on his phone said the same thing.

They held hands, closed their eyes, gathered their thoughts, and offered a prayer that had no words.

Creative Writing Starter One-Hundred-Twenty-Four

Begin writing with: Locks and keys . . .

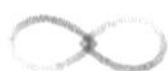

Day One-Hundred-Twenty-Five
Select Calming Strategy Nine or Ten

Creative Writing Setup One-Hundred-Twenty-Five

Let's pinch each other to be sure we are awake and not dreaming.

"Ouch!"

"Ouch!" Okay, we're awake!

They had been talking about this trip for what seemed like forever. Their conversations had started to take on a dream quality for a long time. Here they were, the tickets, reservations, arrangements and travel books were in their hands. The years melted away as they realized their journey had begun.

Creative Writing Starter One-Hundred-Twenty-Five

Begin writing with: Dragging the metal table . . .

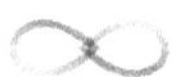

Day One-Hundred-Twenty-Six
Select Calming Strategy Nine or Ten

Creative Writing Setup One-Hundred-Twenty-Six

Three long steps spanned out ten or twelve feet on both sides of the extra large glass and oak double-entry doors. There was plenty of room for gathering outside the building. In the cool of the evening, she sat alone on the middle step, feeling the previous week swirl through her. She could not imagine what tomorrow would be like.

Creative Writing Starter One-Hundred-Twenty-Six

Begin writing with: Leaving his gift behind . . .

Day One-Hundred-Twenty-Seven
Select Calming Strategy Nine or Ten

Creative Writing Setup One-Hundred-Twenty-Seven

Footprints and sand castles, impressions of bodies that had laid sunning on their towels, and holes where umbrellas had been dug deep to provide shade all gave way to the rising tide. All evidence of the day washed away, yet the day had been carried in the hearts of those who had been there. The tide receded, leaving the beach washed and ready for a new day.

Creative Writing Starter One-Hundred-Twenty-Seven

Begin writing with: From the second story window . . .

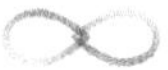

Day One-Hundred-Twenty-Eight
Select Calming Strategy Nine or Ten

Creative Writing Setup One-Hundred-Twenty-Eight

Miles rolled under the tires and rotated the odometer. The time passed without notice as the music, word games, and family stories had them dancing and laughing in their seats.

Creative Writing Starter One-Hundred-Twenty-Eight

Begin writing with: Fresh baked . . .

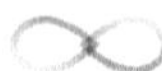

Day One-Hundred-Twenty-Nine
Select Calming Strategy Nine or Ten

Creative Writing Setup One-Hundred-Twenty-Nine

One month ago, moving had not entered her mind. The children were out from school and down with chickenpox—one at a time. But the move had been an answer to her prayer. She did not stop to think about what it would cost her, cost her children. Each day felt like one step forward and one step sideways. Backing up was not considered an option. She pressed on, hoping for the best.

Creative Writing Starter One-Hundred-Twenty-Nine

Begin writing with: Pottery bowls . . .

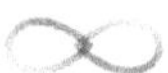

Day One-Hundred-Thirty
Select Calming Strategy Nine or Ten

Creative Writing Setup One-Hundred-Thirty

Sitting on the kitchen floor, utterly focused, her hands pulled, looped, and fumbled as she tried to tie her shoelaces by herself. Her mother cheered her on in silence. Again and again, she kept at it. "I can do this, I know I can do this," she would mutter under her breath whenever it seemed too much for her. All of a sudden, the laces stayed where they were put, and loops held their place. And there it was: a shoelace tied in a sort-of neat bow.

"I did it!"

Creative Writing Starter One-Hundred-Thirty

Begin writing with: They all heard . . .

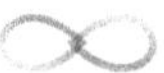

Day One-Hundred-Thirty-One
Select Calming Strategy Nine or Ten

Creative Writing Setup One-Hundred-Thirty-One

Evening provided time for them to read. They had always had a book they were reading together. Today was his turn to read. "Do you know where my glasses are?" he asked from his recliner.

Without looking up, she suggested the table in the living room.

"Looked there. Nothing. I've looked everywhere!"

Looking at him over her glasses, she smiled. "Have you checked your shirt pocket?"

He touched his pocket, then grinned at her. "Time to read, Babe."

Creative Writing Starter One-Hundred-Thirty-One

Begin writing with: Plunged into darkness . . .

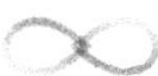

Day One-Hundred-Thirty-Two
Select Calming Strategy Nine or Ten

Creative Writing Setup One-Hundred-Thirty-Two

Telling jokes around the campfire was, like roasting marshmallows, a tradition in their family. Years later, as adults, they would gather at one another's homes and invariably begin retelling those old jokes and taking the marshmallows out to roast.

Creative Writing Starter One-Hundred-Thirty-Two

Begin writing with: Cold drinks . . .

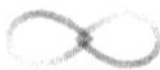

Day One-Hundred-Thirty-Three
Select Calming Strategy Nine or Ten

Creative Writing Setup One-Hundred-Thirty-Three

Tired, hungry and with the car almost on empty, they ventured off the road to find a gas station. It looked like there might be one not too far away. The air grew still and cool as the sun began its descent and fireflies appeared out of nowhere in the tall grasses on either side of the road. They slowed, put their windows down, and enjoyed the spectacle.

Creative Writing Starter One-Hundred-Thirty-Three

Begin writing with: Elevator buttons . . .

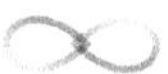

Day One-Hundred-Thirty-Four
Select Calming Strategy Nine or Ten

Creative Writing Setup One-Hundred-Thirty-Four

The potter sat quietly as his hands moved over the lump of clay and his feet set the rhythm of the wheel to his liking. He had no specific plan for this lump, but rather would see what the clay revealed itself to be.

Creative Writing Starter One-Hundred-Thirty-Four

Begin writing with: Slowly, opening . . .

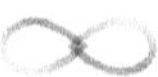

Day One-Hundred-Thirty-Five
Select Calming Strategy Nine or Ten

Creative Writing Setup One Hundred Thirty-Five

Walking the perimeter of the buildings she came upon an odd sight. A door with its handle removed had metal bars fixed in an X across it. The hinges had been soldered to prevent movement. Large pieces of broken concrete, boulders, and old oak beams had been tossed in front of the door. Peeking out from beneath the barriers was a single red flower in full bloom. She saw the promise that one day this door would again be free to open.

Creative Writing Starter One-Hundred-Thirty-Five

Begin writing with: Under glass . . .

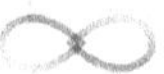

Day One-Hundred-Thirty-Six
Select Calming Strategy Nine or Ten

Creative Writing Setup One-Hundred-Thirty-Six

Dazed by shock and thick smoke, they stumbled out of their home, unaware of the blankets and warm tea offered, caring only that they were safe together.

Creative Writing Starter One-Hundred-Thirty-Six

Begin writing with: Gates closed . . .

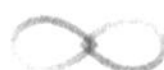

Day One-Hundred-Thirty-Seven
Select Calming Strategy Nine or Ten

Creative Writing Setup One-Hundred-Thirty-Seven

Tapestries hung over windows and in doorways with no doors. A cold draft whistled through the empty hallways, and the large rooms were bare except for a few pieces of furniture huddled around empty fireplaces. The stories this castle would tell her. She set down her bags and got out her pen and notebook.

Creative Writing Starter One-Hundred-Thirty-Seven

Begin writing with: On the back porch . . .

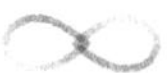

Day One-Hundred-Thirty-Eight
Select Calming Strategy Nine or Ten

Creative Writing Setup One-Hundred-Thirty-Eight

The view from their table at the Tuscan restaurant fed their souls as the food fed their bodies. They heard the voices of the generations of those who worked the olive groves, grape vines, and presses, as they were carried across the years on the breeze that moved out of the valleys and across the hills. They felt the energy that came from the ancient stones in the floor beneath their feet and the wall before them.

Creative Writing Starter One-Hundred-Thirty-Eight

Begin writing with: Stones tossed . . .

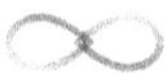

Day One-Hundred-Thirty-Nine
Select Calming Strategy Nine or Ten

Creative Writing Setup One-Hundred-Thirty-Nine

Gingerbread trim and lace curtains graced every building in the little Swiss mountain village. The people in the village had told her, "We just like things this way." But she was sure there were stories of passion, of love, of intrigue and of heroism behind the tidy facades. If there weren't any stories, or none that anyone would admit to, she would make some up to stir the imagination.

Creative Writing Starter One-Hundred-Thirty-Nine

Begin writing with: Crossing the river . . .

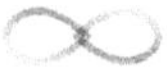

Day One-Hundred Forty
Select Calming Strategy Nine or Ten

Creative Writing Setup One-Hundred-Forty

It's winter break. Sunshine here we come! It's been cold and rainy, not unusual for the time of year, and we are ready, really ready, for some sunshine and swimming in the ocean!

A final check of the bags revealed bathing suits, shorts, t-shirts, sun hats and baseball caps, jeans and a long sleeve shirt. What's this, a heavy sweater? "Okay, toss that on the bed," she said, nodding at the sweater, "We'll leave it here! Let's go!"

Creative Writing Starter One-Hundred-Forty

Begin writing with: The day wore on . . .

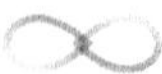

Day One-Hundred-Forty-One
Select Calming Strategy Nine or Ten

Creative Writing Setup One-Hundred-Forty-One

It was their first night in their new home. The movers had not yet arrived, so they had made a quick trip to pick up sleeping bags, pillows, towels, plastic cups, and two nightlights. That last item would help them get a good night's sleep because the kids would sleep better with nightlights in their rooms. Once the kids were in bed, they sat on the front steps and finished the pizza and soda pop and listened to the crickets.

Creative Writing Starter One-Hundred-Forty-One

Begin writing with: Pictures waited to be . . .

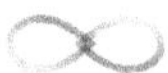

Day One-Hundred-Forty-Two
Select Calming Strategy Nine or Ten

Creative Writing Setup One-Hundred-Forty-Two

One night, as the snow fell outside, he declared aloud to himself, "Tonight I'm going out to play in the snow!" He felt like a kid again. He got dressed, put on his coat, hat, gloves and boots and out he went. It was a good long time before he came back in.

Creative Writing Starter One-Hundred-Forty-Two

Begin writing with: Cornfields . . .

Day One-Hundred-Forty-Three
Select Calming Strategy Nine or Ten

Creative Writing Setup One-Hundred-Forty-Three

They sat without talking on the empty bench. The game was over, the stands empty, but he was not ready to leave. The sun dropped behind the stadium wall and the evening air grew cool. The field light came on as the lone ball player stepped out of the dugout, a broken bat hanging from his loose grip.

Creative Writing Starter One-Hundred-Forty-Three

Begin writing with: The blind man's cane . . .

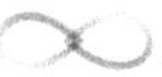

Day One-Hundred-Forty-Four
Select Calming Strategy Nine or Ten

Creative Writing Setup One-Hundred-Forty-Four

News chattered on over the gurgling of the brewing morning coffee and the silence between them. At last she said, "I'd like to take dance lessons."

"What for?" he asked.

Sighing, she replied, "Just to do something."

"Okay, sure," he responded.

She began to fill out the dance application and was soon feeling immensely happy as she wrote in "Tango" as her dance of choice.

Creative Writing Starter One-Hundred-Forty-Four

Begin writing with: She wore a broach . . .

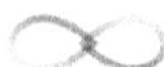

Day One-Hundred-Forty-Five
Select Calming Strategy Nine or Ten

Creative Writing Setup One Hundred Forty-Five

The three blue lights flashed rhythmically below the four that shone steadily. They were amused when they saw their kitten pawing in fascination, trying to catch the lights. They had to pull the plug to give the kitten some relief.

Creative Writing Starter One Hundred Forty-Five

Begin writing with: Dumping the bag . . .

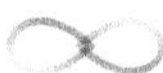

Day One-Hundred-Forty-Six
Select Calming Strategy Nine or Ten

Creative Writing Setup One-Hundred-Forty-Six

Rolling back off the side of the boat into the water, their first task was to get to the shark cage. It was only a few meters away, but with a killer shark nearby it was a long few meters.

Creative Writing Starter One Hundred Forty-Six

Begin writing with: Bird cages for . . .

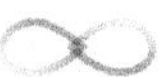

Day One-Hundred-Forty-Seven
Select Calming Strategy Nine or Ten

Creative Writing Setup One-Hundred-Forty-Seven

They met for coffee at a little shop across town. This being the first meeting, she did not want to meet close to her apartment. He sounded nice, a blind date set up by her cousin. "You two will get on well, I'm sure of it," said the woman who could not keep a boyfriend for six months.

She had casually met someone who lived near her, but perhaps it would be nice to get to know this fellow. Entering the coffee shop, there he was.

Creative Writing Starter One Hundred Forty-Seven

Begin writing with: An expert in . . .

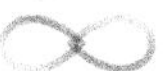

Day One-Hundred-Forty-Eight
Select Calming Strategy Nine or Ten

Creative Writing Setup One Hundred Forty-Eight

There was only one piece of banana cream pie left. They played cards for it, and the old guy won. Looking at his winnings, fork in hand, he paused. He got up and got two more forks and gave them to the two young fellas.

Creative Writing Starter One Hundred Forty-Eight

Begin writing with: The penny jar . . .

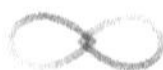

Day One-Hundred-Forty-Nine
Select Calming Strategy Nine or Ten

Creative Writing Setup One-Hundred-Forty-Nine

Funny to have a gift exchange in the summer, but that was Edith for you, always looking for ways to get and keep everyone interested and caring for one another. She was both socially confident and awkward alike. I loved that about her.

Creative Writing Starter One Hundred Forty-Nine

Begin writing with: The catering truck . . .

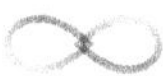

Day One-Hundred-Fifty
Select Calming Strategy Nine or Ten

Creative Writing Setup One-Hundred-Fifty

She placed the cut on the paper drawing so she could make adjustments in the color of glass as she went along. This was to be a large window for the stairwell of a home on the beach. It would light up the stairwell and passersby would see it all day, as it would catch the light from sun up to sundown.

Creative Writing Starter One-Hundred-Fifty

Begin writing with: I read about . . .

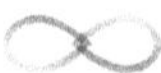

Day One-Hundred-Fifty-One
Select Calming Strategy Eleven or Twelve

Creative Writing Setup One-Hundred-Fifty-One

Behind her childhood home, the melting of winter's snowpack had caused spring's swelling of the creek. The subsequent spot carved out near the footbridge, where the water now stilled under a summer sky, was filled with frogs and tadpoles and had become her playground.

Creative Writing Starter One-Hundred-Fifty-One

Begin writing with: Baseball caps and . . .

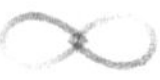

Day One-Hundred-Fifty-Two
Select Calming Strategy Eleven or Twelve

Creative Writing Setup One-Hundred-Fifty-Two

The floodlights coming on were the signal for the skaters to take to the ice. They did not think about the length of time they had to skate. They knew only that when the lights turned off, then on again, it would be time to go. If they stayed, they would soon have to pick their way home by the glow of streetlights alone.

Creative Writing Starter One-Hundred-Fifty-Two

Begin writing with: An ordinary person . . .

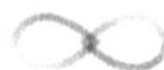

Day One-Hundred-Fifty-Three
Select Calming Strategy Eleven or Twelve

Creative Writing Setup One-Hundred-Fifty-Three

Early dawn sunlight lit their way to the barn. They were late. The milk cows were groaning from the fullness of their udders. The horses were stamping and snorting out of hunger. "Go get Mom and Dad. We'll get a licking, but we need help." He began to relieve the oldest of the dairy cows as his brother rushed off.

Creative Writing Starter One-Hundred-Fifty-Three

Begin writing with: Can you just imagine . . .

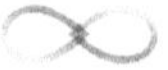

Day One-Hundred-Fifty-Four
Select Calming Strategy Eleven or Twelve

Creative Writing Setup One-Hundred-Fifty-Four

Just as the train pulled into the station, he noticed a family drop down behind the last car onto the tracks and disappear into the darkness. He got on his train home and worked to erase their faces from his mind.

Creative Writing Starter One-Hundred-Fifty-Four

Begin writing with: Instead of new clothes . . .

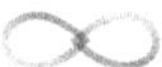

Day One-Hundred-Fifty-Five
Select Calming Strategy Eleven or Twelve

Creative Writing Setup One-Hundred-Fifty-Five

Huge mirrors lined the walls of the hallway. Fingerprints, smudges, and outlines of little faces covered the mirrors at child height. Staff would clean the mirrors periodically but that was so the children could add new fingerprints, smudges and outlines of their faces.

Creative Writing Starter One-Hundred-Fifty-Five

Begin writing with: Her scarf slipped . . .

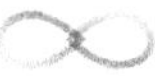

Day One-Hundred-Fifty-Six
Select Calming Strategy Eleven or Twelve

Creative Writing Setup One-Hundred-Fifty-Six

Panning for gold after the snowmelt would often yield a small stash of gold. Well, fool's gold, as the grownups called it. But it was gold to the children all the same. Every spring they were rich!

Creative Writing Starter One-Hundred-Fifty-Six

Begin writing with: During the next three . . .

Day One-Hundred-Fifty-Seven
Select Calming Strategy Eleven or Twelve

Creative Writing Setup One-Hundred-Fifty-Seven

Standing on the bridge of the ship, with the controls at their fingertips, they felt as though the ship beneath their feet was an extension of them and they could command it at will. The commander appeared in the doorway, and their sense of control vanished when they saw him.

Creative Writing Starter One-Hundred-Fifty-Seven

Begin writing with: Through the night . . .

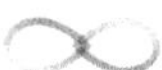

Day One-Hundred-Fifty-Eight
Select Calming Strategy Eleven or Twelve

Creative Writing Setup One-Hundred-Fifty-Eight

Hatboxes piled on top of one another in a corner of the shop and had been there for as long as she had been shopping here. Those who bought hats were given a box, but not one of those. One day the boxes were gone. "Where did the hatboxes go?" she inquired.

"Ah," said the shop owner. "Her Majesty called for them."

"Her Majesty?"

"Yes, those were a few of her hats. We were holding onto them for her," the shop owner said, matter-of-factly.

Creative Writing Starter One-Hundred-Fifty-Eight

Begin writing with: Mother says I'm lucky . . .

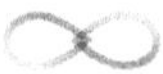

Day One-Hundred-Fifty-Nine
Select Calming Strategy Eleven or Twelve

Creative Writing Setup One-Hundred-Fifty-Nine

Night after night she would lie awake, unable to go to sleep. With only the light from the street lamp across the road, she imagined faces on the ceiling above her. Because the images repeated so often, she gave them names. She told them stories and listened to their stories. Soon, she was eager to go to bed to catch up with her imaginary friends.

Creative Writing Starter One-Hundred-Fifty-Nine

Begin writing with: Over forty . . .

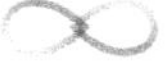

Day One-Hundred-Sixty
Select Calming Strategy Eleven or Twelve

Creative Writing Setup One-Hundred-Sixty

The heavy brocade and velvet curtain separated the pool table and the bar. The bar side of the curtain was swollen with revelers drowning their senses in anything the bartender could pour them. Two men stood surveying the room, their backs against the curtain. One after the other, they slid through the break between the curtain panels. Blinking in disbelief, their eyes met. One checked his watch while the other stared at the room. Were they early or late?

Creative Writing Starter One-Hundred-Sixty

Begin writing with: Forgetting to take . . .

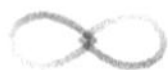

Day One-Hundred-Sixty-One
Select Calming Strategy Eleven or Twelve

Creative Writing Setup One-Hundred-Sixty-One

Stopping by their bedroom doors to listen to her children breathing slowly as they slept, she thought of the day and its ups and downs. She listened to her own heart beating and wondered how in rhythm it was with theirs. Sighing, she went down the stairs. She hoped they would sleep in a little bit tomorrow morning.

Creative Writing Starter One-Hundred-Sixty-One

Begin writing with: Pulling the tablecloth . . .

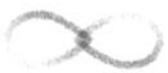

Day One-Hundred-Sixty-Two
Select Calming Strategy Eleven or Twelve

Creative Writing Setup One-Hundred-Sixty-Two

Arms full of stale smelly socks, t-shirts and a pair of jeans that could have stood up in the corner of the room by themselves, she walked down the hallway with her head to one side, trying, without success, to avoid the stale odor of clothes worn too long. She thought of ways to make sure the kids cleaned under their beds, instead of cleaning by stowing everything under their beds.

Creative Writing Starter One-Hundred-Sixty-Two

Begin writing with: From across the valley . . .

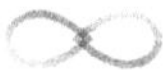

Day One-Hundred-Sixty-Three
Select Calming Strategy Eleven or Twelve

Creative Writing Setup One-Hundred-Sixty-Three

Keys jangled on his hip like bells on a horse's harness. They served two purposes for him. One, if any kids were up to no good, they were warned he was coming and to scram, and the second purpose was that the noise was a kind of music to him, helping him sing when he was alone.

Creative Writing Starter One-Hundred-Sixty-Three

Begin writing with: Red and green motor scooters . . .

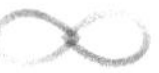

Day One-Hundred-Sixty-Four
Select Calming Strategy Eleven or Twelve

Creative Writing Setup One-Hundred-Sixty-Four

Mesmerized by the swinging of the pendulum on the old grandfather clock in the hallway, they would sit watching the pendulum swinging back and forth, back and forth, as the second hand ticked off the seconds then the minute hand clicked from one minute to the next. The gong at the quarter hour would ready them for the louder gongs at the half hour and the hour. That was before television.

Creative Writing Starter One-Hundred-Sixty-Four

Begin writing with: Lining the dresser . . .

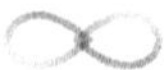

Day One-Hundred-Sixty-Five
Select Calming Strategy Eleven or Twelve

Creative Writing Setup One-Hundred-Sixty-Five

Ten o'clock. She shook her head, hardly believing it was so late. It seemed only a few minutes ago that it was 7:30, the kids had just left for their bus, and she was stepping into the shower. She pulled on her boots and raincoat and walked out into the rain.

Creative Writing Starter One-Hundred-Sixty-Five

Begin writing with: Dropping the hammer . . .

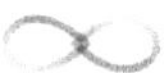

Day One-Hundred-Sixty-Six
Select Calming Strategy Eleven or Twelve

Creative Writing Setup One-Hundred-Sixty-Six

She crept tentatively across the room, as swiftly as she dared, unsure of whether or not the floorboards would bear up under her weight. Reaching the spot where the stairs should be, her heart skipped two beats—there was only an opening and a handrail on the wall.

Creative Writing Starter One-Hundred-Sixty-Six

Begin writing with: Wax had dripped . . .

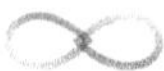

Day One-Hundred-Sixty-Seven
Select Calming Strategy Eleven or Twelve

Creative Writing Setup One-Hundred-Sixty-Seven

Serendipity, some would say outlandish serendipity, had accompanied her during her life. Some said the angels must have kissed her when she was born. Perhaps, but what she knew was that she had an unshakeable knowing that, if she listened to her heart and was fearless, things would work out.

Creative Writing Starter One-Hundred-Sixty-Seven

Begin writing with: A library card . . .

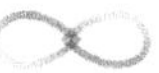

Day One-Hundred-Sixty-Eight
Select Calming Strategy Eleven or Twelve

Creative Writing Setup One-Hundred-Sixty-Eight

At the back of the restaurant, against the wall with the distinctive banana leaf wallpaper, sat two women. The television magnate had her head bent slightly down and to her left as her companion spoke, barely loud enough for the woman to hear while she hastily sketched the idea out onto a storyboard. No drinks, no food, no waiter. No one approached them.

Creative Writing Starter One-Hundred-Sixty-Eight

Begin writing with: Boxes packed and stacked . . .

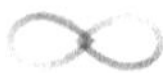

Day One-Hundred-Sixty-Nine
Select Calming Strategy Eleven or Twelve

Creative Writing Setup One-Hundred-Sixty-Nine

In the hot, packed train car, passengers had opened the windows. The two young sisters had taken the ribbons out of their bonnets and held them out the window. One pink and one yellow ribbon played happily in the breeze.

"Don't let go of your ribbons girls," their mother said.

Distracted by her mother's voice, the youngest sister lost hold of her ribbon and they all watched as the line of yellow danced past the windows until it was lost between the cars.

Creative Writing Starter One-Hundred-Sixty-Nine

Begin writing with: Snow fell like . . .

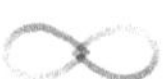

Day One-Hundred-Seventy
Select Calming Strategy Eleven or Twelve

Creative Writing Setup One-Hundred-Seventy

An especially long, nothing-to-do summer day found the children looking to reinvent a use for their tricycles. Turning their tricycles upside down, they sat on the crossbar of the back wheels, gripping the pedals that made the big front wheel go round.

"What are you doing?" their big brother asked.

"Making popcorn, want some?"

Creative Writing Starter One-Hundred-Seventy

Begin writing with: Steps down the side of . . .

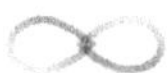

Day One-Hundred-Seventy-One
Select Calming Strategy Eleven or Twelve

Creative Writing Setup One-Hundred-Seventy-One

The dog days of August hit early on the afternoon of July 25th. Their mother drip-dried the children from their baths, laid them down and brought the top sheet up to their necks before she turned on the fan at the end of the hall.

Creative Writing Starter One-Hundred-Seventy-One

Begin writing with: Hanging the paint can on . . .

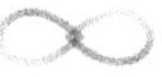

Day One-Hundred-Seventy-Two
Select Calming Strategy Eleven or Twelve

Creative Writing Setup One-Hundred-Seventy-Two

Their car rolled into their driveway at 4:30 on Tuesday afternoon. They were exhausted. They had been on the road since 6:00 that morning, anxious to see their grandchildren, and had pushed through, not even stopping for lunch. The kids heard the car and were at their doors before they got their seatbelts off.

Creative Writing Starter One-Hundred-Seventy-Two

Begin writing with: Turning the lamp on . . .

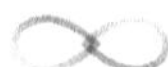

Day One-Hundred-Seventy-Three
Select Calming Strategy Eleven or Twelve

Creative Writing Setup One-Hundred-Seventy-Three

The van's windows, down just a crack, looked a little foggy. *That's odd*, she thought, as she passed by on her way to her car. She stepped back behind her car at the sound of the van's sliding door squeaking open. Out stepped a woman and her little girl. The woman straightened their clothes, combed her hair and the hair of the child, then boosted the little girl into the front seat and buckled her in. The woman then got in the driver's seat of the van and drove away.

Creative Writing Setup One-Hundred-Seventy-Three

Begin writing with: Crackers and cookies . . .

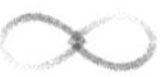

Day One-Hundred-Seventy-Four
Select Calming Strategy Eleven or Twelve

Creative Writing Setup One-Hundred-Seventy-Four

The campfire burned bright and hot in the bitterly cold night. As he got up to put more logs on the fire, his eye caught movement near the truck. "Surely no wildlife would be out on a night like this," he said, just under his breath.

"What's that?"

"Nothing, Mabel." He did not want to worry her with thoughts of wild animals. Bending down to pick up the wood he met two small, smiling eyes.

Creative Writing Starter One-Hundred-Seventy-Four

Begin writing with: Bursting out into . . .

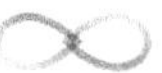

Day One-Hundred-Seventy-Five
Select Calming Strategy Eleven or Twelve

Creative Writing Setup One-Hundred-Seventy-Five

Today, they left extra time to get to the airport. Way more time than necessary perhaps, but their last visit had taught them a lesson. They took a final check around the place to be sure they had not left anything behind this time. Everything was going like clockwork—until they got to airport parking. "Parking Lot Full" read one sign. "Parking Lot Full" read another. They went round and round. There was no parking at all!

Creative Writing Starter One-Hundred-Seventy-Five

Begin writing with: With a handful of . . .

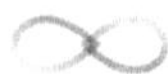

Day One-Hundred-Seventy-Six
Select Calming Strategy Eleven or Twelve

Creative Writing Setup One-Hundred-Seventy-Six

"Remember when Mom first cut her hair?"

"Boy, do I ever!" her younger sister said.

The littlest sister sat quietly.

"Dad hit the roof! He was mad as hell! Mostly because there was nothing he could do about it."

"Yeah, I remember too," the littlest one said. "I remember how pretty she looked."

Creative Writing Starter One-Hundred-Seventy-Six

Begin writing with: Counting the stairs . . .

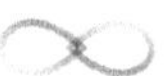

Day One-Hundred-Seventy-Seven
Select Calming Strategy Eleven or Twelve

Creative Writing Setup One-Hundred-Seventy-Seven

She tried and tried to swim to shore but could not figure out why she could not get closer.

"Rip tide. Swim to your right. Rip tide. Swim to your right," she heard someone screaming.

Just as exhaustion was about to set in, an orange rescue float reached her.

Creative Writing Starter One-Hundred-Seventy-Seven

Begin writing with: Whistling and clapping wildly . . .

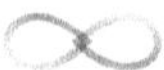

Day One-Hundred-Seventy-Eight
Select Calming Strategy Eleven or Twelve

Creative Writing Setup One-Hundred-Seventy-Eight

Leaving the porch light on, they watched from behind the upstairs bedroom window. Hidden by the curtains, they could see the box marked for donations. It was not long before the family down the street picked it up. Right then, they knew what to do.

Creative Writing Starter One-Hundred-Seventy-Eight

Begin writing with: And best of all . . .

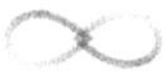

Day One-Hundred-Seventy-Nine
Select Calming Strategy Eleven or Twelve

Creative Writing Setup One-Hundred-Seventy-Nine

The piano played the tunes it was programed to play. The patrons could sing along to their hearts, or liquor's content, and no one got hurt. The former piano player, while safer, sat drowning his sorrows with another shot of whiskey.

Creative Writing Starter One-Hundred-Seventy-Nine

Begin writing with: Maybe next year . . .

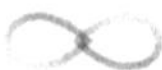

Day One-Hundred-Eighty
Select Calming Strategy Eleven or Twelve

Creative Writing Setup One-Hundred-Eighty

Ballooning had looked exciting, and she had figured it must be safe enough because, after all, the balloons were expensive and incredibly colorful.

They left the valley floor and climbed steadily above the hills into the air currents above. She could see the mountains to her right shrink, bringing the ocean into view. "Breathtaking!" said the woman to her left. Right then, there was a jolt, and the balloon began losing altitude—quickly.

Creative Writing Starter One-Hundred-Eighty

Begin writing with: Putting it off again . . .

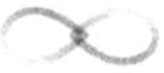

Day One-Hundred-Eighty-One
Select Calming Strategy Thirteen or Fourteen

Creative Writing Setup One-Hundred-Eighty-One

In the light of the setting sun, they walked the sand from the hotel to the pier and back again. The beach was theirs at this time of the day. Almost everyone was either eating dinner or getting ready to go to dinner. They always waited, avoiding the rush, then carried this time with them to sleep.

Creative Writing Starter One-Hundred-Eighty-One

Begin writing with: The journey through . . .

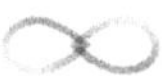

Day One-Hundred-Eighty-Two
Select Calming Strategy Thirteen or Fourteen

Creative Writing Setup One-Hundred-Eighty-Two

He loved having peanut butter and jelly sandwiches every day for lunch. It may have been because he did not like how tuna or egg sandwiches smelled or how the mustard soaked into the bread of the ham sandwiches, but he simply told her he liked them best. There was no discussion that way. He did not like discussions about sandwiches.

Creative Writing Starter One-Hundred-Eighty-Two

Begin writing with: People call me . . .

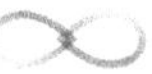

Day One-Hundred-Eighty-Three
Select Calming Strategy Thirteen or Fourteen

Creative Writing Setup One-Hundred-Eighty-Three

Spring brought new life, new hope, and allergies. She had never had allergies before, so it took her a few years before she would admit to having them. For about four weeks she always looked as bad as she felt. Her dad had told her one time that a shot glass of good scotch would cure whatever ailed you. She was sure he meant whatever ailed him, but this year she decided to try it.

Creative Writing Starter One-Hundred-Eighty-Three

Begin writing with: It depended on . . .

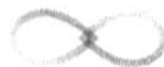

Day One-Hundred-Eighty-Four
Select Calming Strategy Thirteen or Fourteen

Creative Writing Setup One-Hundred-Eighty-Four

She watched her grandfather rolling the newspapers tightly into mini-logs and then line each one up on the row of logs. She noticed he always sat the same way, left leg tucked under and right knee up, that foot flat in front of him, like he was ready to move. She toddled over to him and sat down beside him. He smiled and handed her a roll of paper to play with.

Creative Writing Starter One-Hundred-Eighty-Four

Begin writing with: Shadows inside and out . . .

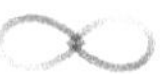

Day One-Hundred-Eighty-Five
Select Calming Strategy Thirteen or Fourteen

Creative Writing Setup One-Hundred-Eighty-Five

It was day two of the cross-country dogsled journey and all was well. The dogs had eaten and slept well the night before and were engrossed in play. Checking the map and the sled's ropes, he whistled. The dogs jockeyed, not for position, for that was determined, but to be harnessed first. He made sure to choose a different dog each time.

Creative Writing Starter One-Hundred-Eighty-Five

Begin writing with: Two oversized rocking chairs and . . .

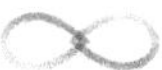

Day One-Hundred-Eighty-Six
Select Calming Strategy Thirteen or Fourteen

Creative Writing Setup One-Hundred-Eighty-Six

Sailing out from the quiet cove into the strong current that would carry them out to sea, he held the rudder firm and watched as the others onboard prepared to unfurl the sails. At just the right time, he would flip the switch, kill the engine, and the sails would drop down and open, catch the wind, and away they would be whisked like a kite high over an open beach.

Creative Writing Starter One-Hundred-Eighty-Six

Begin writing with: Red silk gowns . . .

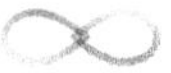

Day One-Hundred-Eighty-Seven
Select Calming Strategy Thirteen or Fourteen

Creative Writing Setup One-Hundred-Eighty-Seven

The roof was pulled off by a lick of the tornado's tail as the windows blew out. The glass doors shattered into a million tiny pieces and sprayed out like bits of ice from a blender. Large pieces of the walls and floor were carried away and dropped in every direction. Only the sounds of the devastation touched the children in the root cellar.

Creative Writing Starter One-Hundred-Eighty-Seven

Begin writing with: Please put on . . .

Day One-Hundred-Eighty-Eight
Select Calming Strategy Thirteen or Fourteen

Creative Writing Setup One-Hundred-Eighty-Eight

An empty fish tank, except for water, bubbled away in the corner.

"Where are the fish?" he asked.

"I don't have any," she responded.

"Why?"

"Because."

"Because why?"

"Just because."

He shook his head and took his drink out onto the patio to enjoy the sunset.

Creative Writing Starter One-Hundred-Eighty-Eight

Begin writing with: The work began . . .

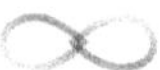

Day One-Hundred-Eighty-Nine
Select Calming Strategy Thirteen or Fourteen

Creative Writing Setup One-Hundred-Eighty-Nine

With the rickety cart at her side, she hovered over the fruit first, picking up one piece at a time. Rolling one at a time in her hands, she eventually selected one that she brought close to her mouth. She then muttered something under her breath before bending her ear towards the fruit. If she smiled and nodded, the piece went in her cart. If she just smiled, the piece went back on the table. It took her a long time, but, once done there, she moved to the vegetables.

Creative Writing Starter One-Hundred-Eighty-Nine

Begin writing with: Really big pool toys . . .

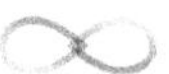

Day One-Hundred-Ninety
Select Calming Strategy Thirteen or Fourteen

Creative Writing Setup One-Hundred-Ninety

She'd run too late to catch the bus, so she called for a ride and sat on the porch to wait. The dew on the roses disappeared. The sunlight moved up the walk to her feet. The neighbor came out in his housecoat to get the morning paper.

Creative Writing Starter One-Hundred-Ninety

Begin writing with: Batteries were dead . . .

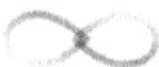

Day One-Hundred-Ninety-One
Select Calming Strategy Thirteen or Fourteen

Creative Writing Setup One-Hundred-Ninety-One

Curled up on their beds, they each read their books until the porch light went out. This was their mother's quiet time when she sat quietly on the porch and had become their adventure time as their books carried them to faraway places.

Creative Writing Starter One-Hundred-Ninety-One

Begin writing with: Baskets of bright . . .

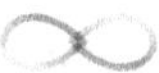

Day One-Hundred-Ninety-Two
Select Calming Strategy Thirteen or Fourteen

Creative Writing Setup One-Hundred-Ninety-Two

This was not a time to be alone. She packed an apple pie and a carton of ice cream, a vase of flowers, and her book. She knocked gently as she let herself in and began making coffee. She set the table while humming childhood songs. They had the pie and coffee in silence. Cleaning up, she hummed more songs, then joined her friend in the living room and read her book in silence.

Creative Writing Starter One-Hundred-Ninety-Two

Begin writing with: Arms full of laundry . . .

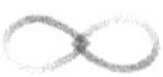

Day One-Hundred-Ninety-Three
Select Calming Strategy Thirteen or Fourteen

Creative Writing Setup One-Hundred-Ninety-Three

The wide-bodied jetliner bound for Los Angeles was near empty. *Plenty of room*, she thought.

An angry voice behind her shouted, "Move!"

A quiet voice said, "No, I would like to sit here."

Soon both the angry and quiet voice were taken off to sort things out.

Neither voice returned.

Creative Writing Starter One-Hundred-Ninety-Three

Begin writing with: With a tip of his hat . . .

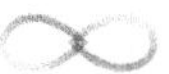

Day One-Hundred-Ninety-Four
Select Calming Strategy Thirteen or Fourteen

Creative Writing Setup One-Hundred-Ninety-Four

With noses red from the cold, they began to sniffle soon after coming inside. She got them into their pajamas, then slippers and housecoats. After wrapping them in blankets, she perched them with hot tea in front of the fireplace. Not long afterwards, they were asleep. There would be no sniffles in the morning.

Creative Writing Starter One-Hundred-Ninety-Four

Begin writing with: You have a tree . . .

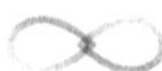

Day One-Hundred-Ninety-Five
Select Calming Strategy Thirteen or Fourteen

Creative Writing Setup One-Hundred-Ninety-Five

Coins and broken crockery covered the bedroom floor. Tossing the hammer aside, he began to count his money. Did he have enough?

Creative Writing Starter One-Hundred-Ninety-Five

Begin writing with: Folding the letter . . .

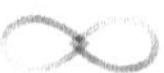

Day One-Hundred-Ninety-Six
Select Calming Strategy Thirteen or Fourteen

Creative Writing Setup One-Hundred-Ninety-Six

The large serving spoon belonged to his mother. They had used it to make cookies together, and her father had used it when making cookies with her. Holding it now, as she mixed the sugar into the butter, she felt her grandmother's and her father's hands holding the bowl.

Creative Writing Starter One-Hundred-Ninety-Six

Begin writing with: Red and green brooms . . .

Day One-Hundred-Ninety-Seven
Select Calming Strategy Thirteen or Fourteen

Creative Writing Setup One-Hundred-Ninety-Seven

The smooth stones on the creek bed were covered with a slimy coating that made them slippery to walk on. Holding onto the bottom of the bridge, then grabbing onto the low-hanging branches, they made their way along the creek to the bank where they had stashed their loot.

Creative Writing Starter One-Hundred-Ninety-Seven

Begin writing with: Determined to find . . .

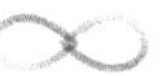

Day One-Hundred-Ninety-Eight
Select Calming Strategy Thirteen or Fourteen

Creative Writing Setup One-Hundred-Ninety-Eight

With sand buckets totally bare of toys and almost empty of sand, the girls now carried buckets of berries, leaves, crab apples, dirt and sticks, and pretended to bake deserts.

Watching them from the kitchen window, their mother was glad the mess was outside.

Creative Writing Starter One-Hundred-Ninety-Eight

Begin writing with: Someone heard the . . .

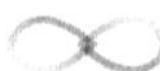

Day One-Hundred-Ninety-Nine
Select Calming Strategy Thirteen or Fourteen

Creative Writing Setup One-Hundred-Ninety-Nine

Twenty-one buses lined the road to the elementary school. It was a big, very big, day. Every student was going on this field trip. Four parents sat aboard each bus—if they had been short one, the whole trip would have been off. With clipboards in hand, teachers gave out nametags then checked and re-checked that names matched the students and their lists. Soon, the principal blew her whistle and the boarding began.

Creative Writing Starter One-Hundred-Ninety-Nine

Begin writing with: She had given them . . .

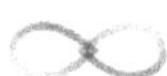

Day Two-Hundred
Select Calming Strategy Thirteen or Fourteen

Creative Writing Setup Two-Hundred

Women in fur coats, wearing dazzling jewels, and men in the finest suits in New York seemed right at home with the bright lights and commotion of the theater's premier show.

From the shadow of a doorway across the street he took it all in. One day he would be one of the finely dressed gentlemen at such a gala event. Checking his watch, he stepped out of the shadows and off to his job of washing dishes at the pizza place.

Creative Writing Starter Two-Hundred

Begin writing with: The one thing . . .

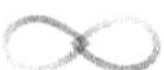

Day Two-Hundred-Two-Hundred-One
Select Calming Strategy Thirteen or Fourteen

Creative Writing Setup Two-Hundred-One

He rolled his truck up to his usual spot by the beach as the sun began to crest the mountains. The weather report had said it would be a sunny day—that meant a good business day for him. This week, he had managed to re-arrange the braces on his truck, making two more boards available for rent. Taking his personal board out from inside the truck, he hit the water to catch some waves before his customers arrived.

Creative Writing Starter Two-Hundred-One

Begin writing with: About ten miles out . . .

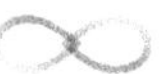

Day Two-Hundred-Two
Select Calming Strategy Thirteen or Fourteen

Creative Writing Setup Two-Hundred-Two

Hidden in the ornate painting's frame was his message. He went as often as he dared to the gallery. He didn't dare try to take any photos. That would draw attention to him and his interest in the painting. Once, he thought a couple had come an unusual number of times, but then realized their meeting was of a personal nature.

In the painting, the woman's intricate-patterned broach caught his eye. He looked back to the frame. Could that be the key?

Creative Writing Starter Two-Hundred-Two

Begin writing with: Every box was open . . .

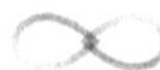

Day Two-Hundred-Three
Select Calming Strategy Thirteen or Fourteen

Creative Writing Setup Two-Hundred-Three

Crouched down on their heels, their little bodies tilted up and down like drinking bird toys, then dipped forward on their toes, back and forth as their eyes and hands sought and plucked treasure coins from the fountain. They put each coin in a neat row between them and when the two lines met they stopped. They changed places and each tossed one coin at a time back into the fountain with wishes of their own.

Creative Writing Starter Two-Hundred-Three

Begin writing with: Bags and bags of . . .

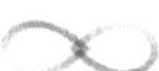

Day Two-Hundred-Four
Select Calming Strategy Thirteen or Fourteen

Creative Writing Setup Two-Hundred-Four

"Prime Retail Space For Lease $25 per sq. ft."

Prime New York real estate, huh? he thought. *Probably next to the dumpster in back of a dive bar on the seedy part of the street. It must be bad for $25 a square foot!* Still, he decided to go have a look. *I'll stop at my friend's place for a drink or two on my way back. I'll have a good story to tell him.* Pulling up in front of the address, he checked the ad twice to be sure he had the right place. He checked his wallet to be sure he had a check. He knew he wanted to rent the place then and there.

Creative Writing Starter Two-Hundred-Four

Begin writing with: Just a small thing . . .

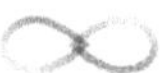

Day Two-Hundred-Five
Select Calming Strategy Thirteen or Fourteen

Creative Writing Setup Two-Hundred-Five

Everything on the street was faded: the paint on the houses, driveways, wooden fences and blinds on the windows. The landscaping looked dried and withered. The desert was reclaiming the area. Yet, on the mailbox halfway down the street, brightly colored balloons swayed in the breeze.

Creative Writing Starter Two-Hundred-Five

Begin writing with: I'd break into a sweat . . .

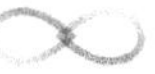

Day Two-Hundred-Six
Select Calming Strategy Thirteen or Fourteen

Creative Writing Setup Two-Hundred-Six

While his paintings would not likely be hung in any famous gallery, the hours he spent painting gave him peace. He would tell her, "I'm going out to splash some paint about with my brushes." This declaration carried two messages. One, "I'm about ready to unravel" and two, "I'll be better when I come back."

She was always glad of the second part.

Creative Writing Starter Two-Hundred-Six

Begin writing with: In the middle of . . .

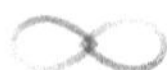

Day Two-Hundred-Seven
Select Calming Strategy Thirteen or Fourteen

Creative Writing Setup Two-Hundred-Seven

The presence of a dozen dogs and their handlers in the customs' area had some wondering, some nervous, and some in a controlled panic. On the hunt for the scent of what, one could only guess, the dogs pushed around and past passengers while their handlers felt their movements through their leash as their eyes were trained on the passengers' reactions.

Creative Writing Starter Two-Hundred-Seven

Begin writing with: Dreams come when . . .

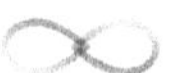

Day Two-Hundred-Eight
Select Calming Strategy Thirteen or Fourteen

Creative Writing Setup Two-Hundred-Eight

"Wicker Chairs and Table For Sale – CHEAP!"

Her porch was bare, except for one cherry tomato plant, so she bought them. Good thing they were inexpensive. She preferred that word. They would do for this season.

Creative Writing Starter Two-Hundred-Eight

Begin writing with: A sunny yellow framed . . .

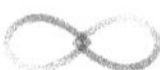

Day Two-Hundred-Nine
Select Calming Strategy Thirteen or Fourteen

Creative Writing Setup Two-Hundred-Nine

Ah, they're home! She wanted to say, "Not again," but something about their heavy steps, baby talk to their dog and cat, and the banging of their front door was funny and comforting at the same time. They were the yang to her yin . . . or something like that. She returned to her reading.

Creative Writing Starter Two-Hundred-Nine

Begin writing with: Planning for five . . .

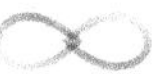

Day Two-Hundred-Ten
Select Calming Strategy Thirteen or Fourteen

Creative Writing Setup Two-Hundred-Ten

The school's March break was on. School bells continued to sound, but no laughing or shouting followed. All was quiet in the schoolyard. Many of her neighbors enjoyed this respite from what they called noise, but she always thought of it as music. She waited eagerly for the kids to come back.

Creative Writing Starter Two-Hundred-Ten

Begin writing with: Somewhere else . . .

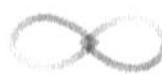

Day Two-Hundred-Eleven
Select Calming Strategy Fifteen or Sixteen

Creative Writing Setup Two-Hundred-Eleven

It got so she had begun stopping at the trash on her way back from the mailbox. There was so much junk mail that she sorted it before coming into the house. She sat down to write letters to the advertisers.

Creative Writing Starter Two-Hundred-Eleven

Begin writing with: Nothing in the suitcase . . .

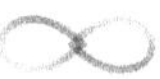

Day Two-Hundred-Twelve
Select Calming Strategy Fifteen or Sixteen

Creative Writing Setup Two-Hundred-Twelve

Huddled together on the curb, they created some shade for their feet by leaning forward over their knees. Still, their bare feet danced sideways as their toes wiggled because of the heat. Their eyes and attention surveyed the road, up and down as far as they could see, watching the steam rise from the road as a light sun shower fell all around them.

Creative Writing Starter Two-Hundred-Twelve

Begin writing with: Between the cotton . . .

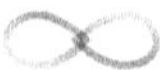

Day Two-Hundred-Thirteen
Select Calming Strategy Fifteen or Sixteen

Creative Writing Setup Two-Hundred-Thirteen

Climbing the steps into the bus, getting change from the driver for the fare, and then holding the overhead rails, she stepped awkwardly down the aisle as the bus lurched into gear and away from the stop. Holding the bag close, she sat poised to pull the bell and get off at her stop.

Creative Writing Starter Two-Hundred-Thirteen

Begin writing with: Work is for . . .

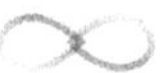

Day Two-Hundred-Fourteen
Select Calming Strategy Fifteen or Sixteen

Creative Writing Setup Two-Hundred-Fourteen

The past month had her head spinning, and her body exhausted from the move, her first in thirteen years. She dropped down into the big chair. The bed would have to wait.

Creative Writing Starter Two-Hundred-Fourteen

Begin writing with: When we fall . . .

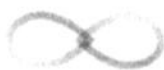

Day Two-Hundred-Fifteen
Select Calming Strategy Fifteen or Sixteen

Creative Writing Setup Two-Hundred-Fifteen

She shook the towels and wet bathing suits out over the lawn then carried them inside and put them into the washing machine. Then, she went back outside to hose down the toys and empty food containers over the driveway, sending the sand in a little stream down the street. The sun began to drop fast as she ushered the kids into the shower to wash sand and salt down the drain. She wondered what of this day would be remembered.

Creative Writing Starter Two-Hundred-Fifteen

Begin writing with: Make sure it is . . .

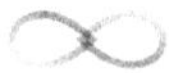

Day Two-Hundred-Sixteen
Select Calming Strategy Fifteen or Sixteen

Creative Writing Setup Two-Hundred-Sixteen

"Don't bang the—"

Bang went the screen door.

Her eyes looked to heaven and she yelled after them with words and a tone she was sure were her mother's.

She laughed about that now, now that the kids were all grown, and the house was silent. Going out into the garden she let the screen door slam.

Creative Writing Starter Two-Hundred-Sixteen

Begin writing with: I can promise . . .

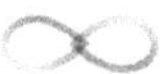

Day Two-Hundred-Seventeen
Select Calming Strategy Fifteen or Sixteen

Creative Writing Setup Two-Hundred-Seventeen

Almost falling down the hill, they went straight for the old tree house. No one knew who had built it, but the big boys took credit and claimed it as their own. Today, the big boys were away, so they would claim it as theirs, even if just for one day. The best part was that the big boys would never know.

Creative Writing Starter Two-Hundred-Seventeen

Begin writing with: This same habit . . .

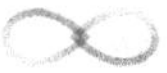

Day Two-Hundred-Eighteen
Select Calming Strategy Fifteen or Sixteen

Creative Writing Setup Two-Hundred-Eighteen

Four months of practicing a song with a two-year-old was both an accomplishment and a significant part of his total life so far. She had taught him and watched him as he sang from the third step from the bottom, their makeshift stage.

Now she watched as he looked out from a real stage into a sea of faces. His face lit up when he found her.

Creative Writing Starter Two-Hundred-Eighteen

Begin writing with: Slow down long enough . . .

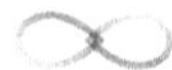

Day Two-Hundred-Nineteen
Select Calming Strategy Fifteen or Sixteen

Creative Writing Setup Two-Hundred-Nineteen

She thought about getting up to make the coffee. She sat up and rubbed her eyes to get used to the darkness. Slipping her feet onto the bare floor, she felt for her slippers. A sigh escaped from deep within her belly.

"Honey, are you okay?" he said.

"Yes, everything is perfect," she heard herself reply from that same place the sigh had come from. Things were perfect now, no longer just fine.

Creative Writing Starter Two-Hundred-Nineteen

Begin writing with: Again and again . . .

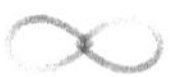

Day Two-Hundred-Twenty
Select Calming Strategy Fifteen or Sixteen

Creative Writing Setup Two-Hundred-Twenty

Periwinkle blue, she thought. *Such a lovely little teapot is just the right size for a good sized cup of tea.* Setting it on the tray beside her favorite chair, she remembered her friend and the many times tea had been a part of their times together. She nibbled at a cookie.

Creative Writing Starter Two-Hundred-Twenty

Begin writing with: Pumpkin seeds . . .

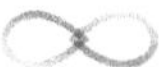

Day Two-Hundred-Twenty-One
Select Calming Strategy Fifteen or Sixteen

Creative Writing Setup Two-Hundred-Twenty-One

Putting her feet up on the porch's waist-high railing, she followed the line of her toes until her eyes reached up into the night sky. She studied the stars. There they were again, the Three Sisters, stars of Orion's belt. She closed her eyes and thought again of her own sisters.

Creative Writing Starter Two-Hundred-Twenty-One

Begin writing with: With a wry laugh . . .

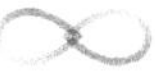

Day Two-Hundred-Twenty-Two
Select Calming Strategy Fifteen or Sixteen

Creative Writing Setup Two-Hundred-Twenty-Two

There was so much mail jammed into her mailbox that the box's door hung down. Sorting through it, she discovered only a week's worth of junk mail. Right then she made a decision. She went inside to write a note to her friend. If no letters came to her, she would send one each day to someone else.

Creative Writing Starter Two-Hundred-Twenty-Two

Begin writing with: Under the basket . . .

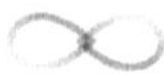

Day Two-Hundred-Twenty-Three
Select Calming Strategy Fifteen or Sixteen

Creative Writing Setup Two-Hundred-Twenty-Three

On trash day, the old man struggled again to get the trashcan to the curb. A school bus rolled up, stopped, and the front door of the bus opened. Two boys jumped down and ran to help. One held the gate open while the other helped pull the can to the curb. Waving and saying "see you later" to the old man, the boys then dashed back to the waiting bus. The driver smiled as they bounded up the steps, then closed the bus door and rolled away.

Creative Writing Starter Two-Hundred-Twenty-Three

Begin writing with: When children use . . .

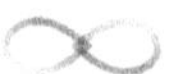

Day Two-Hundred-Twenty-Four
Select Calming Strategy Fifteen or Sixteen

Creative Writing Setup Two-Hundred-Twenty-Four

Lamenting over the size of her yard, she dismissed, for now, her grand outdoor ideas. Sitting down with pen and paper, she looked around and sketched out this yard's perfect design.

Creative Writing Starter Two-Hundred-Twenty-Four

Begin writing with: Bursting through the door . . .

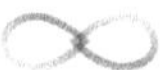

Day Two-Hundred-Twenty-Five
Select Calming Strategy Fifteen or Sixteen

Creative Writing Setup Two-Hundred-Twenty-Five

A vague recollection of wrapping her little hands around a chocolate-dipped ice cream slipped out during the growing silence of the warm summer night. The memory of that treat was a magical experience and she enjoyed every moment.

Creative Writing Starter Two-Hundred-Twenty-Five

Begin writing with: The measure of . . .

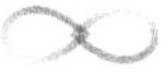

Day Two-Hundred-Twenty-Six
Select Calming Strategy Fifteen or Sixteen

Creative Writing Setup Two-Hundred-Twenty-Six

"Why do you break the bubbles in your pancakes?" her sister-in-law asked. "The bubbles help them cook faster."

That made no sense, so she replied, "Really?" and continued to break the bubbles.

"Well, Dad taught me to make pancakes and that's what he said, but it was probably to keep me from walking away and letting them burn."

They smiled at each other, and her sister-in-law poured more batter and took a turn at breaking the bubbles as the pancakes cooked.

Creative Writing Starter Two-Hundred-Twenty-Six

Begin writing with: Repeating the questions . . .

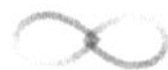

Day Two-Hundred-Twenty-Seven
Select Calming Strategy Fifteen or Sixteen

Creative Writing Setup Two-Hundred-Twenty-Seven

A warm winter day had coaxed the skunks from their den to forage for food. The kids burst onto the rink to play a game of hockey and were stopped short by the sight of a young skunk stuck in the hockey net. They skated slowly back towards the door and called animal control.

Creative Writing Starter Two-Hundred-Twenty-Seven

Begin writing with: Things come up when . . .

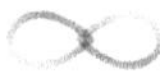

Day Two-Hundred-Twenty-Eight
Select Calming Strategy Fifteen or Sixteen

Creative Writing Setup Two-Hundred-Twenty-Eight

The west wall of the kitchen was made of large plate-glass windows. The mid-day sun and heat, along with the yellow and white of the room, made for one very bright room. Muttering to herself, she said, "This room needs some contrast." She left for town and soon came in with three gallons of the deepest, darkest brown the paint guy could make. She was a bit of a cutting-edge person when she could afford to be.

Creative Writing Starter Two-Hundred-Twenty-Eight

Begin writing with: When time does not . . .

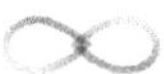

Day Two-Hundred-Twenty-Nine
Select Calming Strategy Fifteen or Sixteen

Creative Writing Setup Two-Hundred-Twenty-Nine

"Okay kids, here we are." Their grandpa lifted them onto the benches of the picnic table where he'd laid pieces of scrap wood, a saw, a hammer, some nails, and pieces of an old sheet. "Time to make us a few boats!"

Handing him nails and holding the pieces of the old sheet was their contribution. Mostly, it was being close to him and creating something. It was not long until everyone was in the water playing with their boats, Grandpa included.

Creative Writing Starter Two-Hundred-Twenty-Nine

Begin writing with: It was not practical . . .

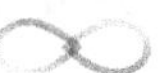

Day Two-Hundred-Thirty
Select Calming Strategy Fifteen or Sixteen

Creative Writing Setup Two-Hundred-Thirty

Her grandchildren brought her gifts from their walks—leaves, sticks, pinecones, rocks, sometimes an old bird's nest—along with stories of the river and creatures they saw. As they told her their stories, she added them to the memories of her own adventures.

Creative Writing Starter Two-Hundred-Thirty

Begin writing with: It was like watching a comedy . . .

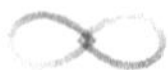

Day Two-Hundred-Thirty-One
Select Calming Strategy Fifteen or Sixteen

Creative Writing Setup Two-Hundred-Thirty-One

"Where is the elephant with an umbrella?" Over and over the children shouted as they jumped up and down, bumping into one another and the countertop.

With both hands in the dishwater, she said, "There is no elephant with an umbrella."

"Yes, yes!" they insisted.

She didn't respond as she rinsed the dishes.

Minutes later they returned. "Here it is. Here is the elephant with an umbrella!" One of them waived the book wildly above his head.

Drying her hands, she said, "Let's read it then!"

Creative Writing Starter Two-Hundred-Thirty-One

Begin writing with: One piece of the . . .

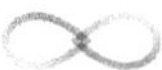

Day Two-Hundred-Thirty-Two
Select Calming Strategy Fifteen or Sixteen

Creative Writing Setup Two-Hundred-Thirty-Two

Holding hands, they walked up and down, counting the steps. Then he closed his eyes and she walked up and down while he counted. Next, it was her turn to close her eyes. Finally, it was time for both of them to close their eyes and go up and down the stairs. Slowly, slowly they did so while their mom watched, ready to respond with assistance or cheers.

Creative Writing Starter Two-Hundred-Thirty-Two

Begin writing with: Finding answers with . . .

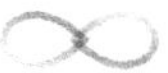

Day Two-Hundred-Thirty-Three
Select Calming Strategy Fifteen or Sixteen

Creative Writing Setup Two-Hundred-Thirty-Three

He slid the bright letters around an imaginary track on the refrigerator door as if they were racecars. The winner stayed, while the loser went into the bowl on the counter. He repeated this until there was only one letter left. Then the basket was emptied back onto the fridge door for another race day.

Creative Writing Starter Two-Hundred-Thirty-Three

Begin writing with: There are hundreds of . . .

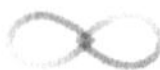

Day Two-Hundred-Thirty-Four
Select Calming Strategy Fifteen or Sixteen

Creative Writing Setup Two-Hundred-Thirty-Four

The house was quiet when they arrived home from school. The girls looked at each other, wondering why there was no noise from their little brother. Maybe he was asleep. They went into the kitchen to get a snack. A loud crash in the backyard caused them to jump. At the top of his lungs, their little brother cried, "It's all right, it's all right, it's all right!" They knew something was not all right! They raced out the back door to see what he had broken this time.

Creative Writing Starter Two-Hundred-Thirty-Three

Begin writing with: Old memories kept . . .

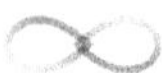

Day Two-Hundred-Thirty-Five
Select Calming Strategy Fifteen or Sixteen

Creative Writing Setup Two-Hundred-Thirty-Five

He sat, obediently watching as lemonade was poured into the large juice jug full of ice. It was the middle of a long hot afternoon and his water was now very warm. He followed the tray of glasses outside. It was not long before patience turned to craftiness as he tried to lick the cool water dripping down the jug onto the tray.

Creative Writing Starter Two-Hundred-Thirty-Five

Begin writing with: Just watching the . . .

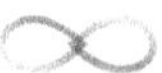

Day Two-Hundred-Thirty-Six
Select Calming Strategy Fifteen or Sixteen

Creative Writing Setup Two-Hundred-Thirty-Six

The littlest one held the plans. "Right then," he said. "Let's first mark off the garden rows."

They picked up stones while he carried the stakes and hammer. He drove in a stake and stepped off to his right. Every two steps, one of the children placed a stone at his heel. At twenty-four steps he stopped, drove in another stake and stepped left. The little crew continued until the garden plot was marked.

"Now for planting!" he said.

The children groaned.

"Right then, tomorrow, the planting!"

Creative Writing Starter Two-Hundred-Thirty-Six

Begin writing with: Walnuts and chocolate . . .

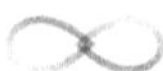

Day Two-Hundred-Thirty-Seven
Select Calming Strategy Fifteen or Sixteen

Creative Writing Setup Two-Hundred-Thirty-Seven

Cleaning mud from his boots, the young lad asked the cook, "Why is that iron chair outside in the middle of the lawn?" The cook ignored him and kept on wiping pastry off the counter. "Why is it not in the barn with the table and the other chairs?" he insisted.

From a stool in the corner, the butler hissed, "Hush! You ask too many questions!" He rose on unsteady legs, grabbed the young man's coat with a surprisingly strong grip, and with fear in his voice said, "And you best stop asking and don't you never go near that chair!"

Creative Writing Starter Two-Hundred-Thirty-Seven

Begin writing with: I am returning to . . .

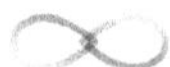

Day Two-Hundred-Thirty-Eight
Select Calming Strategy Fifteen or Sixteen

Creative Writing Setup Two-Hundred-Thirty-Eight

Dragonflies hovered and skimmed over the shallows of the creek. She listened as their wings whispered and watched as the water bubbled its response. People said she was an odd one, but it was the voices of the creatures that she heard—and they said she was perfect.

Creative Writing Starter Two-Hundred-Thirty-Eight

Begin writing with: It was the mission to . . .

Day Two-Hundred-Thirty-Nine
Select Calming Strategy Fifteen or Sixteen

Creative Writing Setup Two-Hundred-Thirty-Nine

Interlopers, all of us, but the streaming site was irresistible, and it was sanctioned by all but the creatures themselves. Prying eyes observed from around the world as the nesting eagles laid their eggs, incubated them, and later fed their little ones.

Creative Writing Starter Two-Hundred-Thirty-Nine

Begin writing with: Looking back over . . .

Day Two-Hundred-Forty
Select Calming Strategy Fifteen or Sixteen

Creative Writing Setup Two-Hundred-Forty

Translating the foreign language text required a small team of us. Gathered at our offices, we stalled almost as soon as we began. We refocused and began again and again. Finally, the intense young man with a moustache spoke up gently. "It's poetry, written in another time. We must let the words come to us like they did for the poet."

Creative Writing Starter Two-Hundred-Forty

Begin writing with: There is no . . .

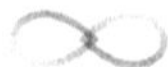

Day Two-Hundred-Forty-One
Select Calming Strategy Seventeen or Eighteen

Creative Writing Setup Two-Hundred-Forty-One

Wide-mouthed hummingbird chicks pushed one another dangerously close to the rim of the rough-hewn nest. Lunch came. They would resume their rivalry later.

Creative Writing Starter Two-Hundred-Forty-One

Begin writing with: Holding the button . . .

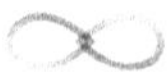

Day Two-Hundred-Forty-Two
Select Calming Strategy Seventeen or Eighteen

Creative Writing Setup Two-Hundred-Forty-Two

Backyard fireworks were drawing to a close. Before the lights came on, there was one last hurrah: the volcano! As the sparks flew up and out with a seeming fury, the little ones stepped behind their parents' legs.

Creative Writing Starter Two-Hundred-Forty-Two

Begin writing with: As a result . . .

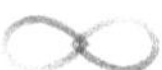

Day Two-Hundred-Forty-Three
Select Calming Strategy Seventeen or Eighteen

Creative Writing Setup Two-Hundred-Forty-Three

The memory in blue ink on the page brought the past before her eyes and touched her heart. She closed the cover. Over the years, she had taken in each day as it had come and let go after it had passed. The sights and sounds of the scene that surrounded her now were from long ago. She lived them again.

Creative Writing Starter Two-Hundred-Forty-Three

Begin writing with: They stuffed the . . .

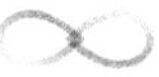

Day Two-Hundred-Forty-Four
Select Calming Strategy Seventeen or Eighteen

Creative Writing Setup Two-Hundred-Forty-Four

Lines everywhere. At first the long line of cars waiting to exit the parking garage irritated her, but then she noticed the mother and her children singing in the car next to her. She began to sing along.

Creative Writing Starter Two-Hundred-Forty-Four

Begin writing with: Spreading the papers . . .

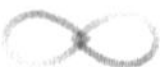

Day Two-Hundred-Forty-Five
Select Calming Strategy Seventeen or Eighteen

Creative Writing Setup Two-Hundred-Forty-Five

Patrons in their seats could see the struggle going on behind the thick red curtains. Silence filled the theatre as all ears strained to hear what was going on. A collective gasp went up as the actors broke through onto the stage and the curtains fell into a heap on top of them.

Creative Writing Starter Two-Hundred-Forty-Five

Begin writing with: The well-ridden wooden horse . . .

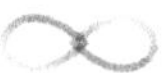

Day Two-Hundred-Forty-Six
Select Calming Strategy Seventeen or Eighteen

Creative Writing Setup Two-Hundred-Forty-Six

They started out on the path, the well-worn one, along the edge of the pine tree grove. After traveling twenty-three minutes along the path, they stepped off to their right through a shadowy opening. In five steps, they found themselves plunged into a forest from before time.

Creative Writing Starter Two-Hundred-Forty-Six

Begin writing with: Pressing flowers...

Day Two-Hundred-Forty-Seven
Select Calming Strategy Seventeen or Eighteen

Creative Writing Setup Two-Hundred-Forty-Seven

Everyone knew where he would be at eight o'clock in the morning: at his desk with two stacks of paper. As his work progressed, the blank pages on his left always became pages filled with words on his right.

Creative Writing Starter Two-Hundred-Forty-Seven

Begin writing with: Autumn leaves spun . . .

Day Two-Hundred-Forty-Eight
Select Calming Strategy Seventeen or Eighteen

Creative Writing Setup Two-Hundred-Forty-Eight

Ideas flew round the table so fast that they were sure many of them had been lost in the attempt to write things down. Still, they were satisfied with what they did get down on paper and were excited about the future.

Creative Writing Starter Two-Hundred-Forty-Eight

Begin writing with: Cutting out the comic strip . . .

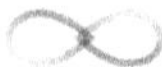

Day Two-Hundred-Forty-Nine
Select Calming Strategy Seventeen or Eighteen

Creative Writing Setup Two-Hundred-Forty-Nine

One day, it struck her that something had changed. Exactly what and when, she could not say. What she could say, if anyone had been there to hear, is that she now got up before the rising of the sun so she could to listen to the world wake up.

Creative Writing Starter Two-Hundred-Forty-Nine

Begin writing with: The biggest bubble ever . . .

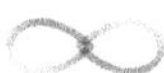

Day Two-Hundred-Fifty
Select Calming Strategy Seventeen or Eighteen

Creative Writing Setup Two-Hundred-Fifty

Ever since she could remember, she loved watching specs of dust float round the room. One day, this is clear in her memory, her mother gave her a dust rag and taught her to clean the dust up. She still loved to help her mom clean.

Creative Writing Starter Two-Hundred-Fifty

Begin writing with: Cinnamon and rosemary . . .

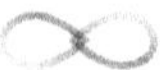

Day Two-Hundred-Fifty-One
Select Calming Strategy Seventeen or Eighteen

Creative Writing Setup Two-Hundred-Fifty-One

Cinnamon sticks, with sprigs of cedar tied on with kitchen string, hung high over the kitchen's large oven. The scent carried a welcome on the currents of heat. That scent, coupled with the heat from the oven, warmed their hearts as well as their bodies.

Creative Writing Starter Two-Hundred-Fifty-One

Begin writing with: The coldest winter . . .

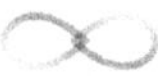

Day Two-Hundred-Fifty-Two
Select Calming Strategy Seventeen or Eighteen

Creative Writing Setup Two-Hundred-Fifty-Two

Unable to tolerate boredom and accepting the invitation of the warm spring day, the older boys, one after the other, jumped out the open windows while the teacher chastised and the younger children watched. The boys headed to the swimming hole and the children back to their penmanship lessons.

Creative Writing Starter Two-Hundred-Fifty-Two

Begin writing with: Making up card games . . .

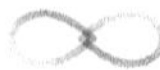

Day Two-Hundred-Fifty-Three
Select Calming Strategy Seventeen or Eighteen

Creative Writing Setup Two-Hundred-Fifty-Three

Absentmindedly gathering their binders, they tossed what was left of their lunches in the trash and stepped out of the practice room for the long walk to the main auditorium where the awards would be given . . . to others.

Creative Writing Starter Two-Hundred-Fifty-Three

Begin writing with: With a brand new . . .

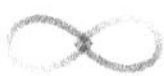

Day Two-Hundred-Fifty-Four
Select Calming Strategy Seventeen or Eighteen

Creative Writing Setup Two-Hundred-Fifty-Four

The string of pearls lay neatly inside the worn purple velvet-lined box. She opened the clasp and secured it at the back of her neck. How often had she seen her mother do this? How often had her mother seen *her* mother do this? She touched the pearls as she left the house.

Creative Writing Starter Two-Hundred-Fifty-Four

Begin writing with: Taking the shortcut . . .

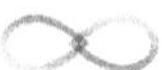

Day Two-Hundred-Fifty-Five
Select Calming Strategy Seventeen or Eighteen

Creative Writing Setup Two-Hundred-Fifty-Five

Methodically snapping each of the pencils in three pieces, some in four pieces, took him about an hour. There were a lot of pencils, but he took his time. With his fingers stained with graphite, he sat playing with the broken pieces for another half hour or so. Looking around, he saw the box of sixty-four crayons.

Creative Writing Starter Two-Hundred-Fifty-Five

Begin writing with: She was not finished . . .

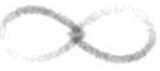

Day Two-Hundred-Fifty-Six
Select Calming Strategy Seventeen or Eighteen

Creative Writing Setup Two-Hundred-Fifty-Six

Windows lined the wall, top to bottom, that overlooked the valley. Neat rows of student desks sat empty. How many hours had they watched the world go by in that room?

Creative Writing Starter Two-Hundred-Fifty-Six

Begin writing with: How does a baby . . .

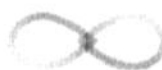

Day Two-Hundred-Fifty-Seven
Select Calming Strategy Seventeen or Eighteen

Creative Writing Setup Two-Hundred-Fifty-Seven

The big beautiful basswood tree had stood for more years than they knew. It was there when the house was built, and they had raised their family as it shaded them against the full sun and composed melodies in the wind and the rain. It spread over the roof now, blocking out the sun the new solar panels required. It would now be used for kindling.

Creative Writing Starter Two-Hundred-Fifty-Seven

Begin writing with: In between the . . .

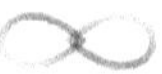

Day Two-Hundred-Fifty-Eight
Select Calming Strategy Seventeen or Eighteen

Creative Writing Setup Two-Hundred-Fifty-Eight

While walking along the boardwalk, the old man would point out places and tell her stories of the famous locals he had beaten at cards, winning everything in their wallets. "It was easy," he said. "They couldn't win at cards to save themselves. I had to stop playing with them because I felt sorry for them. One afternoon he brought out a deck of cards. "Want to play?"

Creative Writing Starter Two-Hundred-Fifty-Eight

Begin writing with: Opening their eyes . . .

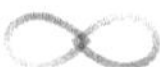

Day Two-Hundred-Fifty-Nine
Select Calming Strategy Seventeen or Eighteen

Creative Writing Setup Two-Hundred-Fifty-Nine

At six o'clock, they gathered at the bottom of the street, just far enough away from the newlywed's house so they could not be seen. The neighbor signaled to them that the newlyweds had left. They quickly set in motion their party plans. By the time the homeowners got back, the backyard was decorated, food and drinks were on the tables, and friends had arrived to welcome them in.

Creative Writing Starter Two-Hundred-Fifty-Nine

Begin writing with: Carrots with their tops . . .

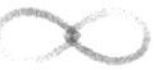

Day Two-Hundred-Sixty
Select Calming Strategy Seventeen or Eighteen

Creative Writing Setup Two-Hundred-Sixty

The young couple next door would rush about every morning. She'd watch them, as they'd pause in front of the mirror inside their front door, smile, stick out their tongues at their own image and then at each other before dashing out the door. She would laugh out loud when they did this. One day, she paused at the mirror in her hallway, smiled, and stuck out her tongue. She laughed back at herself from the mirror. She then dashed out the door.

Creative Writing Starter Two-Hundred-Sixty

Begin writing with: Round and round in a circle . . .

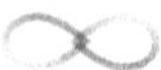

Day Two-Hundred-Sixty-One
Select Calming Strategy Seventeen or Eighteen

Creative Writing Setup Two-Hundred-Sixty-One

Cresting the hill, the lights of the city burned brilliantly before them. There was no stopping here though. They were determined to reach the ocean. The first thing they'd do would be to take off their shoes and dip their feet in, no matter what time of day or night they arrived.

Creative Writing Starter Two-Hundred-Sixty-One

Begin writing with: Is it possible to . . .

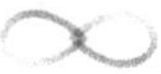

Day Two-Hundred-Sixty-Two
Select Calming Strategy Seventeen or Eighteen

Creative Writing Setup Two-Hundred-Sixty-Two

It did not matter that her shoes were scuffed at the toes and the laces were frayed at their ends: these were her favorite shoes and she wanted to wear them. They looked forward to her growing out of them.

Creative Writing Starter Two-Hundred-Sixty-Two

Begin writing with: Center stage in the . . .

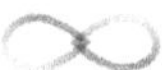

Day Two-Hundred-Sixty-Three
Select Calming Strategy Seventeen or Eighteen

Creative Writing Setup Two-Hundred-Sixty-Three

Knitting a new cap, she thinks of the person who will wear it and knits love and courage into each loop of yarn. This one is a lovely lavender and a deep plum, intended for a woman. She smiles to herself as she thinks, *maybe a man will pick it up?*

Creative Writing Starter Two-Hundred-Sixty-Three

Begin writing with: Caring not that . . .

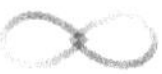

Day Two-Hundred-Sixty-Four
Select Calming Strategy Seventeen or Eighteen

Creative Writing Setup Two-Hundred-Sixty-Four

Sometimes his door was closed, but it was always unlocked. She never saw him lock it. His place was like his heart, always open and ready to greet others. She felt the depth of this gift now that he was gone.

Creative Writing Starter Two-Hundred-Sixty-Four

Begin writing with: From a window at the top of . . .

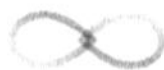

Day Two-Hundred-Sixty-Five
Select Calming Strategy Seventeen or Eighteen

Creative Writing Setup Two-Hundred-Sixty-Five

Some said that all it took was regular watering to make the plants thrive. Yes, water was a key, for sure, but she knew the master key was her whispers that brought out the best in them.

Creative Writing Starter Two-Hundred-Sixty-Five

Begin writing with: In the tradition of . . .

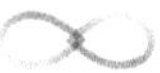

Day Two-Hundred-Sixty-Six
Select Calming Strategy Seventeen or Eighteen

Creative Writing Setup Two-Hundred-Sixty-Six

It must have been the grating of the window being lifted in its frame that drew her attention. She looked across the street to see a fellow thrust himself up onto the windowsill and disappear headfirst into the house. Shaking her head to make sense of this, she went into the house and picked up the phone.

Creative Writing Starter Two-Hundred-Sixty-Six

Begin writing with: Sadly, prizewinners were . . .

Day Two-Hundred-Sixty-Seven
Select Calming Strategy Seventeen or Eighteen

Creative Writing Setup Two-Hundred-Sixty-Seven

Her eyes instantly grew wide and she drew in a deep quick breath. She felt her heart skip a beat at the sight of the largest dictionary she had ever seen. Her grandmother drew up two chairs and they sat down. The old woman then put the impressive tome on the table. Their journey into the world of words had begun.

Creative Writing Starter Two-Hundred-Sixty-Seven

Begin writing with: Faces pressed to the . . .

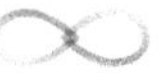

Day Two-Hundred-Sixty-Eight
Select Calming Strategy Seventeen or Eighteen

Creative Writing Setup Two-Hundred-Sixty-Eight

Weathered frames leaned against the cabinet like bits of old wood piled against the side of a shed. They opened the box of family photos. It made sense to put the yellowed and cracked photos in the old frames, but what should they do with the newer family photos in their shiny frames? They would decide later. They went for the hammer and hooks.

Creative Writing Starter Two-Hundred-Sixty-Eight

Begin writing with: Dumping the bag . . .

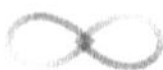

Day Two-Hundred-Sixty-Nine
Select Calming Strategy Seventeen or Eighteen

Creative Writing Setup Two-Hundred-Sixty-Nine

Old mail, open and unopened, newspapers, magazines and parcels, trinkets from New Year's, vacation and birthday announcements were stuffed everywhere in the house: under chairs, beside the bed, on shelves, on the top of drawers, behind the curtains, inside the bathtub . . . they could hardly believe their eyes. They had almost decided to box and toss everything when a pair of pearl earrings fell out of a handkerchief.

Creative Writing Starter Two-Hundred-Sixty-Nine

Begin writing with: Calling her number . . .

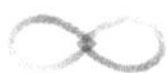

Day Two-Hundred-Seventy
Select Calming Strategy Seventeen or Eighteen

Creative Writing Setup Two-Hundred-Seventy

Before moving away, she visited her old stomping grounds once more. The houses seemed distant, as if being seen from inside a dream. She stopped the car, abruptly, beside an empty field. The old school was gone. So, too, would be the houses, along with her past, when she drove away this time.

Creative Writing Starter Two-Hundred-Seventy

Begin writing with: Blankets draped over . . .

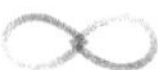

Day Two-Hundred-Seventy-One
Select Calming Strategy Nineteen or Twenty

Creative Writing Setup Two-Hundred-Seventy-One

"Would you like this coat?" the old woman offered.

She didn't want to refuse her, but she also did not want to accept something she did not really like, so she said, "Yes, but are you sure you do not want to keep it?" The desire to not refuse the old woman had won. Giving the old woman a hug, she left with the coat under her arm.

Creative Writing Starter Two-Hundred-Seventy-One

Begin writing with: Playing under the . . .

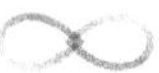

Day Two-Hundred-Seventy-Two
Select Calming Strategy Nineteen or Twenty

Creative Writing Setup Two-Hundred-Seventy-Two

It was time for lunch, and she had not even had breakfast. She looked at what had been accomplished, and then at how much was left to do. As a concession, she grabbed an apple and kept on working.

Creative Writing Starter Two-Hundred-Seventy-Two

Begin writing with: Pulling up to the . . .

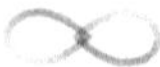

Day Two-Hundred-Seventy-Three
Select Calming Strategy Nineteen or Twenty

Creative Writing Setup Two-Hundred-Seventy-Three

In the early morning, they sat on the two-chair balcony of their familiar hotel room and watched the first shift get things ready for the day. They timed their arrival at breakfast for the freshest food and allowed enough time to chat with the workers.

Creative Writing Starter Two-Hundred-Seventy-Three

Begin writing with: Locking their arms ...

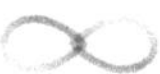

Day Two-Hundred-Seventy-Four
Select Calming Strategy Nineteen or Twenty

Creative Writing Setup Two-Hundred-Seventy-Four

In her mind, she could change the noise coming from the traffic outside to sound more like wind and rain, or ocean waves, than cars and trucks. Closing her eyes, she could imagine the sand and salt air, her bright beach towel, and the warm sun. In this way, she was never far from the beach.

Creative Writing Starter Two-Hundred-Seventy-Four

Begin writing with: Tables at the park . . .

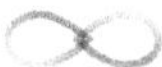

Day Two-Hundred-Seventy-Five
Select Calming Strategy Nineteen or Twenty

Creative Writing Setup Two-Hundred-Seventy-Five

Preparing to visit her friend, she pulled the book from the shelf and a new tea towel from the basket. She put them in her large knitting bag. Making a mental note to stop at the strawberry farm, she put on her sun hat and was on her way.

Creative Writing Starter Two-Hundred-Seventy-Five

Begin writing with: Gluing the mustache in place . . .

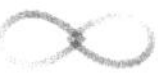

Day Two-Hundred-Seventy-Six
Select Calming Strategy Nineteen or Twenty

Creative Writing Setup Two-Hundred-Seventy-Six

A taste of the big city left her mind and heart reeling. As a small-town girl, she was torn between the comfort and security of her home and the excitement and possibilities of the city. Boarding the plane home, she knew she wanted to come back. Waking the next morning, her excitement about the city felt like a dream and, like a dream, vanished. So did her resolve to venture out again.

Creative Writing Starter Two-Hundred-Seventy-Six

Begin writing with: Dismissing the argument . . .

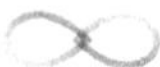

Day Two-Hundred-Seventy-Seven
Select Calming Strategy Nineteen or Twenty

Creative Writing Setup Two-Hundred-Seventy-Seven

Competing interests had everyone at odds with one another. Having been given the task to find a solution, she decided the first question to ask was what each person needed. Like undoing a knot, she found the common thread and followed it.

Creative Writing Starter Two-Hundred-Seventy-Seven

Begin writing with: Take time to . . .

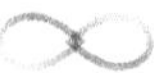

Day Two-Hundred-Seventy-Eight
Select Calming Strategy Nineteen or Twenty

Creative Writing Setup Two-Hundred-Seventy-Eight

It took a long time to collect one-hundred-fifty-seven dollars in coins. Two one-gallon jugs collected the money one coin—sometimes a small handful—at a time. The time had come to buy the bike they'd share. What would they save for next?

Creative Writing Starter Two-Hundred-Seventy-Eight

Begin writing with: None of them fit . . .

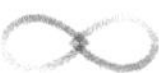

Day Two-Hundred-Seventy-Nine
Select Calming Strategy Nineteen or Twenty

Creative Writing Setup Two-Hundred-Seventy-Nine

Emptied of linen, the cabinet stood ready to be picked up. Not just a piece of furniture, it was a piece of history—their history. Like all history, it would now pass into memory. How would they rewrite this bit of their past?

Creative Writing Starter Two-Hundred-Seventy-Nine

Begin writing with: Removing their shoes . . .

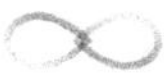

Day Two-Hundred-Eighty
Select Calming Strategy Nineteen or Twenty

Creative Writing Setup Two-Hundred-Eighty

While visiting the old woman's home, she saw a sliver of what looked to be a large mirror almost hidden behind the sideboard in the dining room. It was odd, she thought, that the wall above the sideboard was bare. A mirror would be perfect there. She kept her thoughts to herself.

Creative Writing Starter Two-Hundred-Eighty

Begin writing with: With a dollar in her wallet . . .

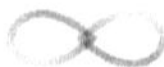

Day Two-Hundred-Eighty-One
Select Calming Strategy Nineteen or Twenty

Creative Writing Setup Two-Hundred-Eighty-One

She drizzled chocolate over fresh pears while everyone chatted excitedly outside. Four of the teenagers came in; arms open wide, each of the boys ready to carry a tray of the desert. Out they went, and the chattering stopped. She wiped her hands and joined them.

Creative Writing Starter Two-Hundred-Eighty-One

Begin writing with: Watching the dog . . .

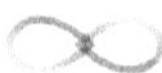

Day Two-Hundred-Eighty-Two
Select Calming Strategy Nineteen or Twenty

Creative Writing Setup Two-Hundred-Eighty-Two

Bicycles, tricycles, Big Wheels and skateboards littered the front yard. From the street, one could guess from the high-pitched sound, that there was a backyard pool and playground teeming with children. As he drove into the garage, he smiled in response to the routine scene.

Creative Writing Starter Two-Hundred-Eighty-Two

Begin writing with: Sliding backs the hidden . . .

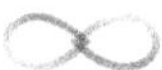

Day Two-Hundred-Eighty-Three
Select Calming Strategy Nineteen or Twenty

Creative Writing Setup Two-Hundred-Eighty-Three

She'd gotten her granddaughter's gift muddled up again. While she would prefer to point to many reasons why, the inescapable truth was becoming apparent. Best she gets a system to take her aging into account. Her sister would know what to do.

Creative Writing Starter Two-Hundred-Eighty-Three

Begin writing with: Throwing the rock down . . .

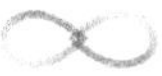

Day Two-Hundred-Eighty-Four
Select Calming Strategy Nineteen or Twenty

Creative Writing Setup Two-Hundred-Eighty-Four

She watched in amazement as the ice in the puddle disappeared. When she came back later that afternoon, the puddle itself was gone. She could hardly believe it!

Creative Writing Starter Two-Hundred-Eighty-Four

Begin writing with: Costumes from another . . .

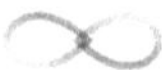

Day Two-Hundred-Eighty-Five
Select Calming Strategy Nineteen or Twenty

Creative Writing Setup Two-Hundred-Eighty-Five

They saw eyes peeking through the window from just over the back of a couch. As they came around the corner from the bus stop on their way home, the children popped up and waved plump little hands. Passing the house, the neighbors smiled and waved back.

Creative Writing Starter Two-Hundred-Eighty-Five

Begin writing with: One more week until . . .

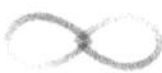

Day Two-Hundred-Eighty-Six
Select Calming Strategy Nineteen or Twenty

Creative Writing Setup Two-Hundred-Eighty-Six

Once in a while, not often enough however, she would fill the bathtub with warm sudsy bubbles and dim the lights, planning to take a relaxing twenty-minute soak. Once in, she would begin to think, often aloud, of things she had to get done. Stubbornly she would stay—she was going to relax! Soon the thinking would grow quieter, the list of things to do would grow thinner and she would relax.

Creative Writing Starter Two-Hundred-Eighty-Six

Begin writing with: Viewing the ornate . . .

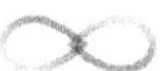

Day Two-Hundred-Eighty-Seven
Select Calming Strategy Nineteen or Twenty

Creative Writing Setup Two-Hundred-Eighty-Seven

For no reason, no reason at all, she would open and close the cupboard doors in the office kitchen. She wondered why, and would often ask herself why, but no answer came. It bothered others, so she only did it when no one else was there.

Creative Writing Starter Two-Hundred-Eighty-Seven

Begin writing with: Across the ocean . . .

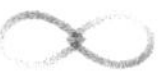

Day Two-Hundred-Eighty-Eight
Select Calming Strategy Nineteen or Twenty

Creative Writing Setup Two-Hundred-Eighty-Eight

One day she put on a large pot of coffee, filled a fruit bowl full of strawberries, and broke up a dark chocolate bar on a plate. Putting them in the center of the table, she sipped and nibbled on these all day long.

Creative Writing Starter Two-Hundred-Eighty-Eight

Begin writing with: Prying the lid off . . .

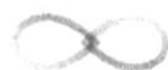

Day Two-Hundred-Eighty-Nine
Select Calming Strategy Nineteen or Twenty

Creative Writing Setup Two-Hundred-Eighty-Nine

Muddy footprints went from the garden, over the grass, and onto the walkway, up the steps, and ended at the empty rain boots that set at the back door. Inside, the boot's owner had been carried to the bath, clothes and all, while they all laughed as she told them about the squirrel she had chased.

Creative Writing Starter Two-Hundred-Eighty-Nine

Begin writing with: Not a day older . . .

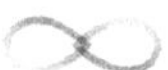

Day Two-Hundred-Ninety
Select Calming Strategy Nineteen or Twenty

Creative Writing Setup Two-Hundred-Ninety

She loved sitting at the big table, on its high chairs. Oblivious to her parents' nervousness, she wiggled, stood up and sat down, as though she was sitting in her little chair. From this chair, she could see things on the high shelves, and she liked the things on the high shelves.

Creative Writing Starter Two-Hundred-Ninety

Begin writing with: Taping the sign . . .

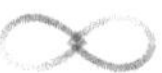

Day Two-Hundred-Ninety-One
Select Calming Strategy Nineteen or Twenty

Creative Writing Setup Two-Hundred-Ninety-One

He heard his neighbor knocking. She called out, "I need some help getting an umbrella upstairs, are you free?"

"Sure," he said. Looking into the back of her van, his enthusiasm waned. "We need the moving dolly and another strong back," he said.

She gave him a confused look.

"Lady, this kind of umbrella is not easily carried up a flight of stairs." He made a call and waited for his friend to arrive.

Creative Writing Starter Two-Hundred-Ninety-One

Begin writing with: Stumbling into . . .

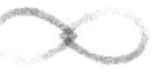

Day Two-Hundred-Ninety-Two
Select Calming Strategy Nineteen or Twenty

Creative Writing Setup Two-Hundred-Ninety-Two

Their families were in different cities, but they had it neatly worked out. Every other year they would visit one of the other's families together, and the next year they would each visit their own family on their own. This year they were ready for their separate trips.

Creative Writing Starter Two-Hundred-Ninety-Two

Begin writing with: Pushing the cart . . .

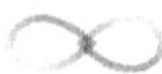

Day Two-Hundred-Ninety-Three
Select Calming Strategy Nineteen or Twenty

Creative Writing Setup Two-Hundred-Ninety-Three

Apple pies were in the oven when they noticed there was no vanilla ice cream in the freezer. "Did you check the big freezer in the basement?" Grandpa asked.

"Yes," they chimed in unison.

Picking up his keys, he said, "Okay, pile into the car. Let's go get some vanilla ice cream."

A voice from the living room said, "Maybe some chocolate too?"

Creative Writing Starter Two-Hundred-Ninety-Three

Begin writing with: His idea seemed . . .

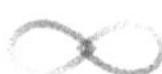

Day Two-Hundred-Ninety-Four
Select Calming Strategy Nineteen or Twenty

Creative Writing Setup Two-Hundred-Ninety-Four

It was late, and the paper was almost complete. The only things to do were the finishing touches: checking the word count and running a spell check. She decided to finish in the morning.

Waking in a panic, she ran to the computer. It was off. She had left it on and forgotten to plug it in. Plugging it in, the hourglass came up. She hoped for the best.

Creative Writing Starter Two-Hundred-Ninety-Four

Begin writing with: High school kids look . . .

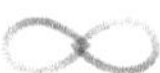

Day Two-Hundred-Ninety-Five
Select Calming Strategy Nineteen or Twenty

Creative Writing Setup Two-Hundred-Ninety-Five

Ready, set, go! All thought of being in the starting block, of the crowds in the stands, and of other runners vanished. Only the finish line was in mind and in view. All she could feel was the finish ribbon across her chest and trailing behind her. Then, the crowd's cheering could be heard.

Creative Writing Starter Two-Hundred-Ninety-Five

Begin writing with: Doing this first . . .

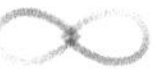

Day Two-Hundred-Ninety-Six
Select Calming Strategy Nineteen or Twenty

Creative Writing Setup Two-Hundred-Ninety-Six

Being late was unusual for her. In fact, her lateness was actually due to circumstances outside her control. No explanation would be asked for, so she relaxed, slowed down, and was glad she had enjoyed having had this time playing in the rain with her son.

Creative Writing Starter Two-Hundred-Ninety-Six

Begin writing with: Bees swarming . . .

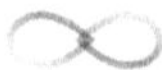

Day Two-Hundred-Ninety-Seven
Select Calming Strategy Nineteen or Twenty

Creative Writing Setup Two-Hundred-Ninety-Seven

Plunk, plunk, plunk. Water dripped on her head from the hole in the gutter where the old downspout had been. They had forgotten, neglected—it didn't matter which—to attach a new downspout. She pulled the planter under the hole. For now, the water would not go to waste.

Creative Writing Starter Two-Hundred-Ninety-Seven

Begin writing with: Counting the towels . . .

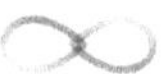

Day Two-Hundred-Ninety-Eight
Select Calming Strategy Nineteen or Twenty

Creative Writing Setup Two-Hundred-Ninety-Eight

About ten yards from the dock, everyone on the raft had jumped into the boat and headed off to town. The towels they left behind would have to wait for them to come back.

Creative Writing Starter Two-Hundred-Ninety-Eight

Begin writing with: Colors of in the night . . .

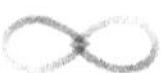

Day Two-Hundred-Ninety-Nine
Select Calming Strategy Nineteen or Twenty

Creative Writing Setup Two-Hundred-Ninety-Nine

As soon as she decided, really decided, she signed up, paid the registration fee, and began her training for the marathon in earnest. She met a few friends, and her training got easier. Well, not exactly easier, but she looked forward to the early morning runs now, which helped a lot.

Creative Writing Starter Two-Hundred-Ninety-Nine

Begin writing with: Mornings in her everyday life . . .

Day Three-Hundred
Select Calming Strategy Nineteen or Twenty

Creative Writing Setup Three-Hundred

The children gathered around the spigot and worked together to fill the water balloons. It took them a bit, but in a while they had the big bucket full of filled water balloons. In a fraction of that time, the bucket was empty, the lawn covered with broken water balloons, and they were drying themselves off with towels.

Creative Writing Starter Three-Hundred

Begin writing with: Down the center of the road . . .

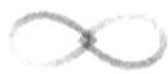

Day Three-Hundred-One
Select Calming Strategy Twenty-One or Twenty-Two

Creative Writing Setup Three-Hundred-One

Looking at the email, she knew right away that he was angry. Pushing herself up from her desk to make a cup of coffee, she noticed the photo she kept under the keyboard. Taking a deep breath, she began to type her reply.

Creative Writing Starter Three-Hundred-One

Begin writing with: The critters scattered . . .

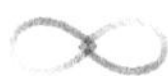

Day Three-Hundred-Two
Select Calming Strategy Twenty-One or Twenty-Two

Creative Writing Setup Three-Hundred-Two

Small talk was really getting under her skin. Her irritation had been growing for a few weeks. One person, Alice, seemed to notice she did not join in conversations. One day, when others were out for lunch, Alice pulled up a chair beside her desk, smiled, and handed her a brown lunch bag.

"Time," Alice said, "to eat. Talk if you want, or not, but you must eat."

Creative Writing Starter Three-Hundred-Two

Begin writing with: Bottles lined the . . .

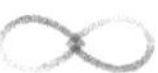

Day Three-Hundred-Three
Select Calming Strategy Twenty-One or Twenty-Two

Creative Writing Setup Three-Hundred-Three

Moving the new shelf into the office meant making room for it first. The lamp table and lamp had to be moved to the left of the door because there was no outlet on the right side. Irritated, she turned to put the lamp down on the desk and tripped over the leg of the cord, breaking the lamp. She moved the table to the right side of the door.

Creative Writing Starter Three-Hundred-Three

Begin writing with: Living without . . .

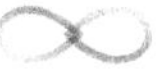

Day Three-Hundred-Four
Select Calming Strategy Twenty-One or Twenty-Two

Creative Writing Setup Three-Hundred-Four

From the street, they could see the window blinds go up and down, up and down, but they never saw anyone pulling a cord. Watching in amusement, they soon noticed three little kids running one way, then the other, as the blinds went up and down.

As a neighbor walked by, she laughed and said, "They love pushing the button that makes the blinds work."

Creative Writing Starter Three-Hundred-Four

Begin writing with: The platter slipped . . .

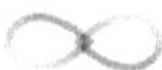

Day Three-Hundred-Five
Select Calming Strategy Twenty-One or Twenty-Two

Creative Writing Setup Three-Hundred-Five

She always thought being born in the year of the rooster ought to have given her some kind of "loves to get up early" benefit. But no. Instead, she would growl at anyone who tried to wake her up before she was good and ready. Perhaps there was some mistake and she really should have been born in the year of the tiger.

Creative Writing Starter Three-Hundred-Five

Begin writing with: Always chattering . . .

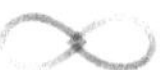

Day Three-Hundred-Six
Select Calming Strategy Twenty-One or Twenty-Two

Creative Writing Setup Three-Hundred-Six

She had to admit it, her hair looked great, amazing actually, but it had taken a lot longer than she had the time to spend. As she got close to her car, her heart sank—and a lot more time than she had put on the parking meter!

Creative Writing Starter Three-Hundred-Six

Begin writing with: We suspected . . .

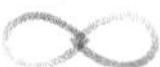

Day Three-Hundred-Seven
Select Calming Strategy Twenty-One or Twenty-Two

Creative Writing Setup Three-Hundred-Seven

Words failed her when walking the cobblestone streets of the small town. She stood at the window of the bookbinder's shop, closed her eyes, and pictured another era with flowing robes, funny shoes and flamboyant hats. So real was her imagination that, upon opening her eyes, she was genuinely surprised to see herself back in her own time.

Creative Writing Starter Three-Hundred-Seven

Begin writing with: Making their kite out of . . .

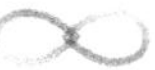

Day Three-Hundred-Eight
Select Calming Strategy Twenty-One or Twenty-Two

Creative Writing Setup Three-Hundred-Eight

After dropping one side of the table, shoving it against the wall, and tightening the net on both sides, she turned to get a paddle and bucket of balls. She intended to spend the afternoon practicing her backhand—she had to win the tournament next month.

Creative Writing Starter Three-Hundred-Eight

Begin writing with: In the old survival handbook . . .

Day Three-Hundred-Nine
Select Calming Strategy Twenty-One or Twenty-Two

Creative Writing Setup Three-Hundred-Nine

"Have you been in the pool very much?" he asked.

"Not yet, I've been busy," she replied. Did that sound as hollow to him as it had to her? She loved the pool. Why had she not been swimming? Come morning, if she had no good reason not to, she would go first thing.

Creative Writing Starter Three-Hundred-Nine

Begin writing with: Books filled with . . .

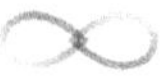

Day Three-Hundred-Ten
Select Calming Strategy Twenty-One or Twenty-Two

Creative Writing Setup Three-Hundred-Ten

They had lived there for five months and had enjoyed only hummingbirds, sparrows and crows—no flies. But today, a fly, a big black fly, flew in as she opened the back door. It was late, and they were tired. She remembered her father using beer and a light to catch flies at the old cottage. With no beer in the house, she poured a cup of milk, put a small lamp on the table and turned it on, shut the door and hoped for the best—or the worst from the fly's point of view.

Creative Writing Starter Three-Hundred-Ten

Begin writing with: We cannot hear you . . .

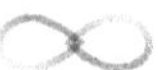

Day Three-Hundred-Eleven
Select Calming Strategy Twenty-One or Twenty-Two

Creative Writing Setup Three-Hundred-Eleven

A parcel sat neatly up against the wall, just inside the gate. The driver must have been short, either in arm's length or time. She smiled. No problem. She turned her attention to the label to see whom it was from. Good thing she had not picked it up, she was sure she would have dropped it. It was from her childhood friend.

Creative Writing Starter Three-Hundred-Eleven

Begin writing with: Doing something about . . .

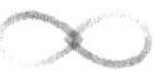

Day Three-Hundred-Twelve
Select Calming Strategy Twenty-One or Twenty-Two

Creative Writing Setup Three-Hundred-Twelve

It was time, time to go. She had come and gone from that house so many times, greeted visitors and wished them well on their way, sat on the front porch with her mom and dad. She sighed. It was time to go and the kids waited in the car, excited. Locking the door, she called out with a smile in her voice, "Coming!"

Creative Writing Starter Three-Hundred-Twelve

Begin writing with: It is not exactly . . .

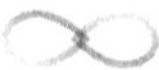

Day Three-Hundred-Thirteen
Select Calming Strategy Twenty-One or Twenty-Two

Creative Writing Setup Three-Hundred-Thirteen

Art class was crowded. The teacher was busy with others, so she went to her easel, put up her canvas, clipped the photo above, unpacked her paints and brushes, and stood back to survey the work thus far. Focusing on the figure in the distance she started to paint.

Creative Writing Starter Three-Hundred-Thirteen

Begin writing with: One thing we all . . .

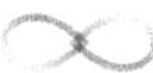

Day Three-Hundred-Fourteen
Select Calming Strategy Twenty-One or Twenty-Two

Creative Writing Setup Three-Hundred-Fourteen

Cracks were appearing in the dashboard of her car. It was an old car and, she supposed, it was to be expected. Eventually, cracks happen. Even so, she hoped she could find something to repair them. It did not escape her that it was a little like hoping moisture cream could turn aged skin into youthful skin. Still, she would try.

Creative Writing Starter Three-Hundred-Fourteen

Begin writing with: What if there were no . . .

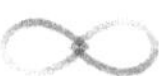

Day Three-Hundred-Fifteen
Select Calming Strategy Twenty-One or Twenty-Two

Creative Writing Setup Three-Hundred-Fifteen

Attachment to animals eluded her. She simply did not understand it. One day, that changed. She witnessed a child finding an abandoned puppy on the street. She saw the connection happen, the child's love going out to a puppy that had, most likely, known only hunger and cold. She knew about the love a child holds in his or her heart.

Creative Writing Starter Three-Hundred-Fifteen

Begin writing with: It can simply be . . .

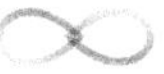

Day Three-Hundred-Sixteen
Select Calming Strategy Twenty-One or Twenty-Two

Creative Writing Setup Three-Hundred-Sixteen

How many to-do lists can a person have? Exasperated, she collected the bits of paper with reminders scratched on them. Sifting through them, the complaining chatter in her mind gave way to the chirping chickadee outside in the cold. There were years of lists; absolutely years of them. Things long since accomplished, fixed, purchased. Her heart opened.

Creative Writing Starter Three-Hundred-Sixteen

Begin writing with: With markers in hand . . .

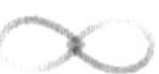

Day Three-Hundred-Seventeen
Select Calming Strategy Twenty-One or Twenty-Two

Creative Writing Setup Three-Hundred-Seventeen

The workstations were clean and in order. All the ducks were lined up, as the boss liked to say. Satisfied, she turned off the lights for the night.

Creative Writing Starter Three-Hundred-Seventeen

Begin writing with: She always said . . .

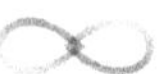

Day Three-Hundred-Eighteen
Select Calming Strategy Twenty-One or Twenty-Two

Creative Writing Setup Three-Hundred-Eighteen

Spilling milk always seemed more about the loss of the money paid for the milk and the adult's inability to control him than anything else. Being the spiller of the milk meant at least a tongue-lashing and often banishment from the table while the adult sopped up the loss and rinsed it down the drain.

Creative Writing Starter Three-Hundred-Eighteen

Begin writing with: There will be time . . .

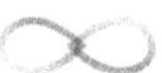

Day Three-Hundred-Nineteen
Select Calming Strategy Twenty-One or Twenty-Two

Creative Writing Setup Three-Hundred-Nineteen

Blue is everywhere: the sky, the water, and her eyes. Baby boys wear lots of blue, although she and her sister have lots of blue dresses. There are blue jeans, blue shirts, blue shoes, blue paint, blue cars, blue couches and tablecloths. Someone got it wrong when applying "blue" to a person whose spirit was low. She would use blue to lift them up.

Creative Writing Starter Three-Hundred-Nineteen

Begin writing with: Most of us don't . . .

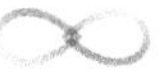

Day Three-Hundred-Twenty
Select Calming Strategy Twenty-One or Twenty-Two

Creative Writing Setup Three-Hundred-Twenty

With her top three number-one choices checked, she began leafing through the summer catalog of classes at the community center. Swimming, ceramics and yoga— all three were there. Which one would end up being her number one choice?

Creative Writing Starter Three-Hundred-Twenty

Begin writing with: Say that way . . .

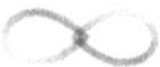

Day Three-Hundred-Twenty-One
Select Calming Strategy Twenty-One or Twenty-Two

Creative Writing Setup Three-Hundred-Twenty-One

Which piñata to choose? There was a shark, a shell, a star, a donkey, a mermaid, and a dinosaur. They were all so wonderful! She chose the star piñata. It was the most colorful and it had streamers hanging from each point, as if it was waving at her.

Creative Writing Starter Three-Hundred-Twenty-One

Begin writing with: Emptiness filled the . . .

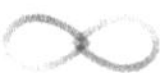

Day Three-Hundred-Twenty-Two
Select Calming Strategy Twenty-One or Twenty-Two

Creative Writing Setup Three-Hundred-Twenty-Two

She wrapped the just-finished scarf in a piece of tissue paper that had been saved from someone's gift. There was no time to stop for new paper. She knew it would be okay because her mom would know that the scarf, and the wrapping of it, had been done by her own hands.

Creative Writing Starter Three-Hundred-Twenty-Two

Begin writing with: Finding Superman's cape . . .

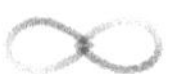

Day Three-Hundred-Twenty-Three
Select Calming Strategy Twenty-One or Twenty-Two

Creative Writing Setup Three-Hundred-Twenty-Three

When she was big, she would plant a rose garden with lavender, sage, and geraniums to accent the roses. For now, her garden was a picture on her bedroom wall. But that was a good start.

Creative Writing Starter Three-Hundred-Twenty-Three

Begin writing with: Let's see what parts . . .

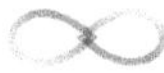

Day Three-Hundred-Twenty-Four
Select Calming Strategy Twenty-One or Twenty-Two

Creative Writing Setup Three-Hundred-Twenty-Four

Awards filled a room in their home. They were all active people and often successful in whatever competitions happened in their town. Some were individual awards, some team awards. One team award stood out. It was the "Family Go-Fish Card Game Tournament" first-place award, composed of four Jokers. That experience was the most fun they'd had all year long.

Creative Writing Starter Three-Hundred-Twenty-Four

Begin writing with: Beads and red ribbon . . .

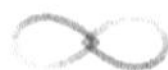

Day Three-Hundred-Twenty-Five
Select Calming Strategy Twenty-One or Twenty-Two

Creative Writing Setup Three-Hundred-Twenty-Five

Bathing suits, flip-flops and towels lined the shelves of the hall closet. Beach bags filled with hats, sunglasses, sunscreen, lip-gloss, and water bottles hung from hooks in the hallway. They were all set for their vacation.

Creative Writing Starter Three-Hundred-Twenty-Five

Begin writing with: The quiet strength . . .

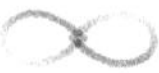

Day Three-Hundred-Twenty-Six
Select Calming Strategy Twenty-One or Twenty-Two

Creative Writing Setup Three-Hundred-Twenty-Six

For five minutes at breakfast, and again at dinner, they played the "I wonder" game. Each would suggest an "I wonder . . ." then decide on one to follow-up on. One morning the littlest one said, "I wonder what would happen if my teacher forgot to give us homework today?" They all laughed. The oldest sister said, "That's not an 'I wonder' but an 'I hope.' I think you just made up a new game for us to play!"

Creative Writing Starter Three-Hundred-Twenty-Six

Begin writing with: Each child got . . .

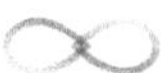

Day Three-Hundred-Twenty-Seven
Select Calming Strategy Twenty-One or Twenty-Two

Creative Writing Setup Three-Hundred-Twenty-Seven

Over the years she had gotten used to telling little fibs about why she wasn't eating much, or not eating at all, when out at friends' places. They had accepted that she was a picky eater and let it go at that. Recently though, she noticed more nutritious food showing up on the tables.

Creative Writing Starter Three-Hundred-Twenty-Seven

Begin writing with: I smiled but had . . .

Day Three-Hundred-Twenty-Eight
Select Calming Strategy Twenty-One or Twenty-Two

Creative Writing Setup Three-Hundred-Twenty-Eight

The garage was definitely getting smaller. Bit by bit, the space around the cars got a little tighter . . . a little like when her jeans got tighter. Time to lose some stuff. She hoped losing stuff was easier than losing weight.

Creative Writing Starter Three-Hundred-Twenty-Eight

Begin writing with: Happy to go . . .

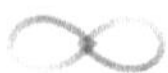

Day Three-Hundred-Twenty-Nine
Select Calming Strategy Twenty-One or Twenty-Two

Creative Writing Setup Three-Hundred-Twenty-Nine

"I've got a paper to write, and I have no idea where to begin!" The rising pitch of the voice let her know to be patient, very patient.

"When is it due?" she replied.

"Ultimately, in a few months, but I have to submit my progress in stages. The first part is due Monday."

Irma said, "Okay, what is the subject?"

"I have no idea. That's the subject! Can you imagine?" The pitch of her daughter's voice had grown so high and loud that Irma had to pull the phone away from her ear.

Creative Writing Starter Three-Hundred-Twenty-Nine

Begin writing with: We called them . . .

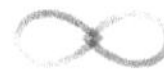

Day Three-Hundred-Thirty

Select Calming Strategy Twenty-One or Twenty-Two

Creative Writing Setup Three-Hundred-Thirty

The idyllic lifestyle here was oddly unsettling. Turning a newly fallen leaf over in her hand, she thought it looked like it should have fallen months ago, at the beginning of winter not in the spring. She mused that the environment affected even the trees in dulling their sensitivity to the need to act.

Creative Writing Starter Three-Hundred-Thirty

Begin writing with: They were also given . . .

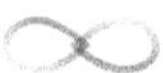

Day Three-Hundred-Thirty-One
Select Calming Strategy Twenty-Three or Twenty-Four

Creative Writing Setup Three-Hundred-Thirty-One

Rolling up her shirtsleeve to show the guest, she declared, "I have an owie."

Bending toward the arm, the lady said, "My what a lot of bandages. Only one owie?"

"It's a long one. Mommy kissed it better and I chose the flower Band-Aids," she said proudly, then pulled her shirtsleeve back down and ran off to the swings.

Creative Writing Starter Three-Hundred-Thirty-One

Begin writing with: All the nice toys . . .

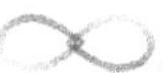

Day Three-Hundred-Thirty-Two
Select Calming Strategy Twenty-Three or Twenty-Four

Creative Writing Setup Three-Hundred-Thirty-Two

Laying obvious questions to one side and resisting the impulse to jump in and sort the situation out, she asked, "Can I get in on this little project?"

The kids, up to their elbows and covered in flour and butter, smiled and said, "No thanks. You go back to bed. We are making you a surprise!"

Without a word, she slowly turned and went back upstairs.

Creative Writing Starter Three-Hundred-Thirty-Two

Begin writing with: She carried the . . .

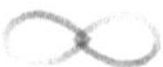

Day Three-Hundred-Thirty-Three
Select Calming Strategy Twenty-Three or Twenty-Four

Creative Writing Setup Three-Hundred-Thirty-Three

She held the large metal bowl up and stared through the rusty holes on the bottom and sides. Sighing, she placed it back on its decorative base. She'd realized, too late, that clearly this was not intended to be an outside piece.

Creative Writing Starter Three-Hundred-Thirty-Three

Begin writing with: I see you have my . . .

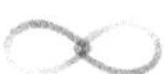

Day Three-Hundred-Thirty-Four
Select Calming Strategy Twenty-Three or Twenty-Four

Creative Writing Setup Three-Hundred-Thirty-Four

From the back door along the path that led to their lookout over the valley, she followed a sparse line of smooth white stones. She had chores to do but felt compelled to follow the stones to their end. Finding her neighbor at the lookout, she scolded her, saying, "There are chores to be done!"

Taking her arm, her friend said, "I know, but let's look at the view for just a few minutes."

Creative Writing Starter Three-Hundred-Thirty-Four

Begin writing with: The motorcycle pulled away . . .

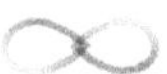

Day Three-Hundred-Thirty-Five
Select Calming Strategy Twenty-Three or Twenty-Four

Creative Writing Setup Three-Hundred-Thirty-Five

Each pot was different, and each plant was, too. At lunch, she would sit at her window and watch them drink up the sun and water. They did not say anything, or did they? She began to imagine what they might be saying. Lunchtime was her favorite part of the workday.

Creative Writing Starter Three-Hundred-Thirty-Five

Begin writing with: Two steps at a time . . .

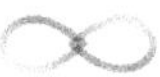

Day Three-Hundred-Thirty-Six
Select Calming Strategy Twenty-Three or Twenty-Four

Creative Writing Setup Three-Hundred-Thirty-Six

"Are you sure?" the driver asked.

Looking from the paper to the storefronts, she said, "Yes, this is the address. Thank you."

He stopped the car.

She tipped him and got out. He hesitated when pulling away from the curb and called out, "Lady, are you sure you're sure?"

"Yes, thanks." The area seemed a bit dodgy, but she felt safe enough. Stepping to the nearest storefront, she opened the door into one of the most welcoming and delightful shops she had been in.

Creative Writing Starter Three-Hundred-Thirty-Six

Begin writing with: There was room for . . .

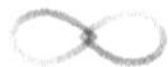

Day Three-Hundred-Thirty-Seven
Select Calming Strategy Twenty-Three or Twenty-Four

Creative Writing Setup Three-Hundred-Thirty-Seven

She found herself walking home past midnight. This part of the city had gone to bed at least two hours ago. The only lights were streetlights and a few porch lights. If anyone was up, they were behind tightly shuttered windows and closed curtains. She breathed in the quiet night air.

Creative Writing Starter Three-Hundred-Thirty-Seven

Begin writing with: Looking away from . . .

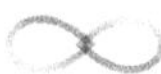

Day Three-Hundred-Thirty-Eight
Select Calming Strategy Twenty-Three or Twenty-Four

Creative Writing Setup Three-Hundred-Thirty-Eight

Checking the mirrors and putting the car in reverse, they backed up, all the while keeping them in their view in the rear-view mirror as the couple waved goodbye.

Creative Writing Starter Three-Hundred-Thirty-Eight

Begin writing with: Following a busy day . . .

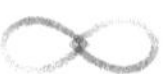

Day Three-Hundred-Thirty-Nine
Select Calming Strategy Twenty-Three or Twenty-Four

Creative Writing Setup Three-Hundred-Thirty-Nine

Her favorite seat was in the basement of the old building, in the large room opposite the window wells. All she could see were feet, well shoes and boots really, whether it was raining, snowing, or sunny. She recognized the people by what they had on their feet. There was one pair of shoes that came by once in a while that she did not know. She loved the stories she made up about this person's shoes.

Creative Writing Starter Three-Hundred-Thirty-Nine

Begin writing with: Kicking the dirt with . . .

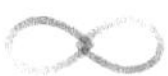

Day Three-Hundred-Forty
Select Calming Strategy Twenty-Three or Twenty-Four

Creative Writing Setup Three-Hundred-Forty

Sitting on the fence, they watched the workers pour the lumpy concrete onto the driveway. That result was not much better than the stones that had been there. Then the workers brought out flat tools and smoothed the bumps, leaving just enough height to help the water drain off.

Creative Writing Starter Three-Hundred-Forty

Begin writing with: For weeks I thought . . .

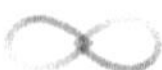

Day Three-Hundred-Forty-One
Select Calming Strategy Twenty-Three or Twenty-Four

Creative Writing Setup Three-Hundred-Forty-One

Books in the children's section looked like they needed to be tidied up. There was a lot of space on the shelves, and, to most people, it was hard to make sense of the order. But all was in perfect order. The children needed to feel free to pick up and put back books as they wanted to. After hours, the librarians would gladly return the area to some order—but not too much.

Creative Writing Starter Three-Hundred-Forty-One

Begin writing with: I walked on . . .

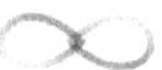

Day Three-Hundred-Forty-Two
Select Calming Strategy Twenty-Three or Twenty-Four

Creative Writing Setup Three-Hundred-Forty-Two

The weight of the silver hand-mirror surprised her. It was a lot heavier than she would have guessed. She could see how there would be some concern that a small child might pick it up. Because of this, it was kept towards the back of the tabletop.

Creative Writing Starter Three-Hundred-Forty-Two

Begin writing with: Making the final turn . . .

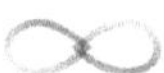

Day Three-Hundred-Forty-Three
Select Calming Strategy Twenty-Three or Twenty-Four

Creative Writing Setup Three-Hundred-Forty-Three

"Could you fit in just one more outfit?" the woman asked.

"Yes, we can," they said without looking at the trunk. If they had, they would have doubted and that would have made it harder to work everything in. The woman left, and they set about fitting the rest of the clothing inside.

Creative Writing Starter Three-Hundred-Forty-Three

Begin writing with: Over everything . . .

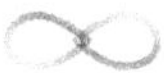

Day Three-Hundred-Forty-Four
Select Calming Strategy Twenty-Three or Twenty-Four

Creative Writing Setup Three-Hundred-Forty-Four

"Yes," he said, "pencils leave a lot less dust on your hands. They make a lot less mess, but they do not possess the softness and ability to create the vision on paper that you have in your mind."

"Ahh, okay, so they are limiting," the student replied.

"Exactly. Now go use what you need to as you create your work of art."

Creative Writing Starter Three-Hundred-Forty-Four

Begin writing with: Opening the study door . . .

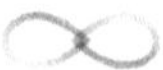

Day Three-Hundred-Forty-Five
Select Calming Strategy Twenty-Three or Twenty-Four

Creative Writing Setup Three-Hundred-Forty-Five

Mike, the golden retriever, stood watch over the seed potatoes. He watched as she began to drop a potato and cover it, then move onto the next. He waited until she had passed him, then fell in behind her, digging them up. At the end of the row, she turned to survey her efforts and instead surveyed his efforts.

Creative Writing Starter Three-Hundred-Forty-Five

Begin writing with: Purchasing one more . . .

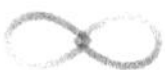

Day Three-Hundred-Forty-Six
Select Calming Strategy Twenty-Three or Twenty-Four

Creative Writing Setup Three-Hundred-Forty-Six

It was not long after she began to pretend to read her books aloud, repeating the words she remembered, that she picked up her mother's book. After a long time of leafing back and forth, she put it down and brought one of her books over to her mother.

"Here, Mommy, this one is much prettier."

Creative Writing Starter Three-Hundred-Forty-Six

Begin writing with: Blocking the sun with . . .

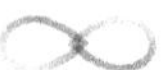

Day Three-Hundred-Forty-Seven
Select Calming Strategy Twenty-Three or Twenty-Four

Creative Writing Setup Three-Hundred-Forty-Seven

If it is possible to describe two dogs barking as though carrying on a conversation, that would have been the two dogs next door. They sounded just like two old people carrying on a conversation. Mentioning this to the owner one day, she said, "Oh yes, and don't try to interrupt them. They'll both snarl at you, and then go back to their conversation. They remind me so much of my parents!"

Creative Writing Starter Three-Hundred-Forty-Seven

Begin writing with: Sitting behind the driver . . .

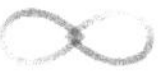

Day Three-Hundred-Forty-Eight
Select Calming Strategy Twenty-Three or Twenty-Four

Creative Writing Setup Three-Hundred-Forty-Eight

Before heading out, they were working out what memento they would bring back. "Something easy to find, useful, and easy to carry home," he suggested, emphasizing the easy-to-carry-home part. He thought, *this time, she'll be stumped.* They were travelling to Italy to visit their first grandchild.

She held up a sketchbook and box of colored pencils and smiled. "We'll wet the baby's hands and feet, press them on the pages, and trace them with the pencils."

Creative Writing Starter Three-Hundred-Forty-Eight

Begin writing with: Taking a few steps . . .

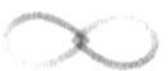

Day Three-Hundred-Forty-Nine
Select Calming Strategy Twenty-Three or Twenty-Four

Creative Writing Setup Three-Hundred-Forty-Nine

"Sometimes it works and sometimes it doesn't." It used to bug them that he said that about so many things: fixing a toaster, hanging pictures, starting the lawnmower . . . so many things. Everything always worked. Well they almost always did.

"Why do you say that, Grandpa?"

"In case it doesn't work, then I will look for a solution instead of getting upset."

"You're smart, Grandpa."

"I don't know about that, but I am glad when things work."

Creative Writing Starter Three-Hundred-Forty-Nine

Begin writing with: Take as many . . .

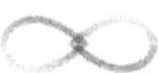

Day Three-Hundred-Fifty
Select Calming Strategy Twenty-Three or Twenty-Four

Creative Writing Setup Three-Hundred-Fifty

Early in the morning and early in the evening, when the light was like looking through a thin haze just before or after a heavy rain, buildings, cars, and streets seemed to slide into the background while trees, flowers, and creatures stepped forward to be noticed, to gently remind me of their beauty as they reflected the brilliance of the light that put them center stage.

Creative Writing Starter Three-Hundred-Fifty

Begin writing with: There are wagons and . . .

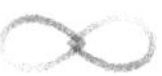

Day Three-Hundred-Fifty-One
Select Calming Strategy Twenty-Three or Twenty-Four

Creative Writing Setup Three-Hundred-Fifty-One

Closing her eyes, she said, "Read me what you wrote."

Her companion began. "In the stillness of the darkness, there is a whisper that holds you there, waiting patiently, no matter how long, for the dawn of the new day."

"Excellent, thank you." Picking up her white cane, she said, "We're quite a team you and me!"

Creative Writing Starter Three-Hundred-Fifty-One

Begin writing with: The table set for . . .

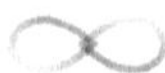

Day Three-Hundred-Fifty-Two
Select Calming Strategy Twenty-Three or Twenty-Four

Creative Writing Setup Three-Hundred-Fifty-Two

She felt sure the front room was bigger than the back room and said so, emphatically, to everyone there.

They got out the tape measure and measured: they were both the same size.

"That's crazy," she said.

"An optical illusion," he said. "The living room's high ceiling makes it look bigger."

Creative Writing Starter Three-Hundred-Fifty-Two

Begin writing with: Making the delivery . . .

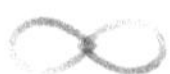

Day Three-Hundred-Fifty-Three
Select Calming Strategy Twenty-Three or Twenty-Four

Creative Writing Setup Three-Hundred-Fifty-Three

One would do the "across" clues and the other the "down" clues. They worked two crosswords at the same time. Pages passed back and forth as one or both needed a clue from the other. The only time they spoke was when commenting on the delicious coffee, the beautiful azaleas, or the scampering squirrels.

Creative Writing Starter Three-Hundred-Fifty-Three

Begin writing with: Now two pieces of . . .

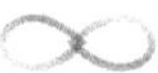

Day Three-Hundred-Fifty-Four
Select Calming Strategy Twenty-Three or Twenty-Four

Creative Writing Setup Three-Hundred-Fifty-Four

Sitting at the traffic light, drivers honked and honked, waving irritably at each other. She waved back. The driver she'd waved at shrugged his shoulders and smiled. It didn't bother him, and she couldn't see what the fuss was about, so it didn't bother her.

Creative Writing Starter Three-Hundred-Fifty-Four

Begin writing with: There were no . . .

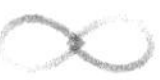

Day Three-Hundred-Fifty-Five
Select Calming Strategy Twenty-Three or Twenty-Four

Creative Writing Setup Three-Hundred-Fifty-Five

He stood back about four feet and greeted her through the locked screen door. The sky was overcast, and the air was damp. There was not apparent value in pondering the implications of the current moment, so she wished him good day and carried on down the street.

Creative Writing Starter Three-Hundred-Fifty-Five

Begin writing with: Staring up at . . .

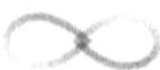

Day Three-Hundred-Fifty-Six
Select Calming Strategy Twenty-Three or Twenty-Four

Creative Writing Setup Three-Hundred-Fifty-Six

The shearing whine of the gas-powered tree saw sounded angry as it was pressed into the trunk. Only the density of the once thriving tree gave the saw, and its wielder, any resistance. The other trees, and the woman in the window, stood as silent witnesses, offering no resistance either.

Creative Writing Starter Three-Hundred-Fifty-Six

Begin writing with: Art begins with . . .

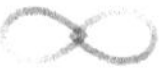

Day Three-Hundred-Fifty-Seven
Select Calming Strategy Twenty-Three or Twenty-Four

Creative Writing Setup Three-Hundred-Fifty-Seven

Gathered around the ring of stones in the field miles from town, they turned their flashlights off, one at a time, and watched as the stars grew brighter and brighter. When there was only the light from the moon and stars, they began speaking, their voices made clearer and sharper by the darkness.

Creative Writing Starter Three-Hundred-Fifty-Seven

Begin writing with: Instantly I saw . . .

Day Three-Hundred-Fifty-Eight
Select Calming Strategy Twenty-Three or Twenty-Four

Creative Writing Setup Three-Hundred-Fifty-Eight

Her journey began by looking at the angora sweaters, full cotton skirts, white socks and white and black shoes worn by the girls in the cracked photograph. All three of them smiled back at her with eyes that remembered from a time before she had words.

Creative Writing Starter Three-Hundred-Fifty-Eight

Begin writing with: In these past . . .

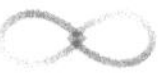

Day Three-Hundred-Fifty-Nine
Select Calming Strategy Twenty-Three or Twenty-Four

Creative Writing Setup Three-Hundred-Fifty-Nine

Sinking into the loose mesh of the chair on the back porch, she wondered how old it was. The cord that laced the mesh to the chair's frame was dangerously close to breaking. Running her hand under the seat, she sighed with relief. *I won't have far to fall if this breaks now,* she thought. *It's almost on the ground.*

Creative Writing Starter Three-Hundred-Fifty-Nine

Begin writing with: A half-cup of . . .

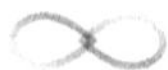

Day Three-Hundred-Sixty
Select Calming Strategy Twenty-Three or Twenty-Four

Creative Writing Setup Three-Hundred-Sixty

Slipping, like lemmings, into the frigid water in the pre-dawn hours, they stood swaying in rhythm together. In response to some unheard call, they all stopped and turned to face a boat that had appeared as though out of nowhere. Then, at the crack of a pistol, they dove in unison into the morning's challenge.

Creative Writing Starter Three-Hundred-Sixty

Begin writing with: In daily life there . . .

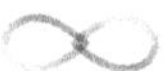

Day Three-Hundred-Sixty-One
Select Calming Strategy Twenty-Three or Twenty-Four

Creative Writing Setup Three-Hundred-Sixty-One

They got up on their knees on the chairs, cleared a space, crossed their arms in front of themselves and leaned in over the puzzle pieces scattered across the tabletop. One by one, they turned the pieces face up, then pulled the straight-edged pieces to the outside edges of the table. Their work had begun.

Creative Writing Starter Three-Hundred-Sixty-One

Begin writing with: So many times . . .

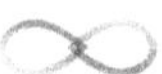

Day Three-Hundred-Sixty-Two
Select Calming Strategy Twenty-Three or Twenty-Four

Creative Writing Setup Three-Hundred-Sixty-Two

The letter on her front door handle was a long laundry list of rules for living here. An old seed of discontent bubbled up, irritating her and prompting a quiet tirade of pushback comments. She read the letter again, feeling just as discontented. Making a cup of tea, she put her legs up for a bit.

Creative Writing Starter Three-Hundred-Sixty-Two

Begin writing with: They never dreamed . . .

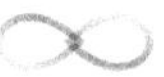

Day Three-Hundred-Sixty-Three
Select Calming Strategy Twenty-Three or Twenty-Four

Creative Writing Setup Three-Hundred-Sixty-Three

Three easy steps to your dream backyard! the book proclaimed.

"This would be fun," she said, nudging him with her elbow.

"What dear?" he said, picking up a computer book.

"Fixing the backyard," she said, waving the book in front of him.

"Yes, yes it would." He would come to regret that response.

Creative Writing Starter Three-Hundred-Sixty-Three

Begin writing with: That particular number of . . .

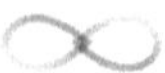

Day Three-Hundred-Sixty-Four
Select Calming Strategy Twenty-Three or Twenty-Four

Creative Writing Setup Three-Hundred-Sixty-Four

Her boss left, suddenly. There were stories, but no one really knew why. She kept her thoughts to herself. A few weeks later, her boss returned, and more stories surfaced. She still kept her thoughts to herself. One day, her boss stopped by her desk and said quietly, "Thank you."

She replied, "You're welcome." She continued to keep her thoughts to herself.

Creative Writing Starter Three-Hundred-Sixty-Four

Begin writing with: In any one direction . . .

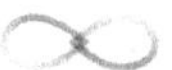

Day Three-Hundred-Sixty-Five
Select Calming Strategy Twenty-Three or Twenty-Four

Creative Writing Setup Three-Hundred-Sixty-Five

It amused her to see the old couple fumble to open the lock. All they had to do was follow the dog and cats in through the broken boards in the wall. Curious, she looked inside and watched them move slowly around the clean, sparse one-room cabin.

"We still like it," they said, spying her. "It was our first home."

Creative Writing Starter Three-Hundred-Sixty-Five

Begin writing with: The power to . . .

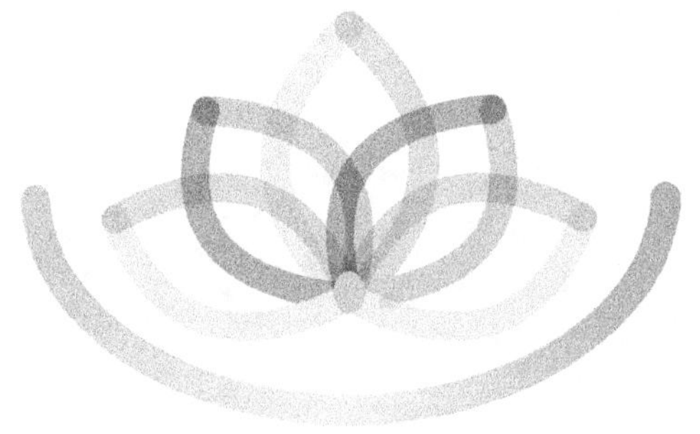

Moving Forward

NELSON / JONES

Moving Forward

We hope you have experienced the power of successfully internalizing the process and experiencing the calming strategies and creative writing prompts. These have the power to guide you toward your personal writing goals. Through your participation, the calming strategies, setups, and starters have become part of your daily routine. As you continue your writing practice, you will find it is now easier to write than not write. In addition, you may notice benefits from the *Nurturing Your Writing Calm* practice spilling gifts into other areas of your life.

Given your achievement, take a few minutes to relish your success. Look over your writing pages and highlight those days that brought excitement, enthusiasm, curiosity, or wonder to your life. Take some time to jot down the day and the reason the writing was meaningful.

If you have yet to begin writing a larger work after using the *Nurturing Your Writing Calm* process, you have a refreshing experience ahead of you. *Nurturing Your Writing Calm* cultivates a powerful connection with your truest self. This creative writing experience fosters your motivation to develop a sustainable writing practice.

Your *Nurturing Your Writing Calm* accomplishment is one of many steps toward fulfilling your ultimate writing goals. What is next for you? How will you use this daily practice to enhance your life? How will you incorporate this daily practice into a meaningful and fulfilling writing future?

What's Next

Please continue your daily writing practice with the tools and processes you have learned. Enter a calm-alert state—be present in your body, engage your senses, find inspiration in the world around you, start your timer, and write.

If, after the 365 days are finished, you would like to continue working with *Nurturing Your Writing Calm*, return to a preferred calming strategy and choose setups and starters from anywhere in the book. You will be amazed and delighted at how your imagination takes you on new adventures.

The *Nurturing Your Writing Calm* book is here to assist you as your grow in your creativity and in your ongoing writing. Below are some ideas about how you can continue your writing practice.

- Return to calming strategies, setups and starters again without referencing your previous writing.

- As you revisit, notice how your imagination takes you on new paths.

- Be conscious about the intersection points between the calming strategies, the setups, and the starters.

- Get together with a friend and share some of your writing from *Nurturing Your Writing Calm*.

- On www.nurturingyourwriterscalm.com there is a complementary video walking through the first five days of *Nurturing Your Writing Calm*.

- After you have experienced *Nurturing Your Writing Calm,* we would invite you to go to Amazon and submit a review. We'd love to receive an email from you sharing your review. You may go to: reviews@nurturingyourwriterscalm.com

- Visit our website for additional resources related to calming and creative writing.

About
the Contributors

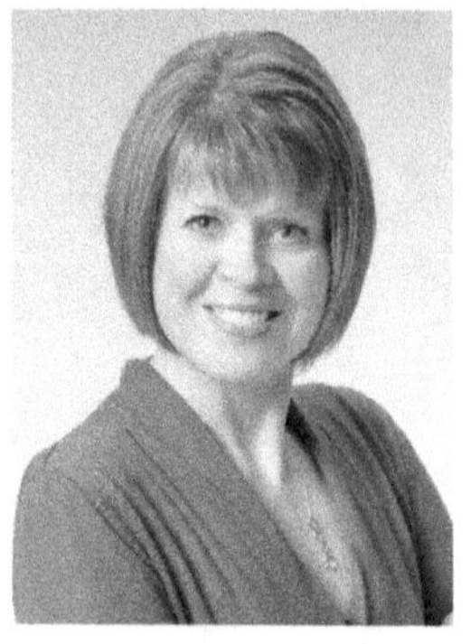

CORALEE A. NELSON is a licensed helping professional, speaker, and educator. She is passionate about supporting people who have walked through difficult life circumstances. One of her favorite ways to do this is to assist people in finding their personal calm so they can integrate a sense of peacefulness into their creative passions. Coralee's proudest accomplishment is raising two wonderful, compassionate, and spirited boys. Coralee lives in Canada with her amazingly understanding husband.

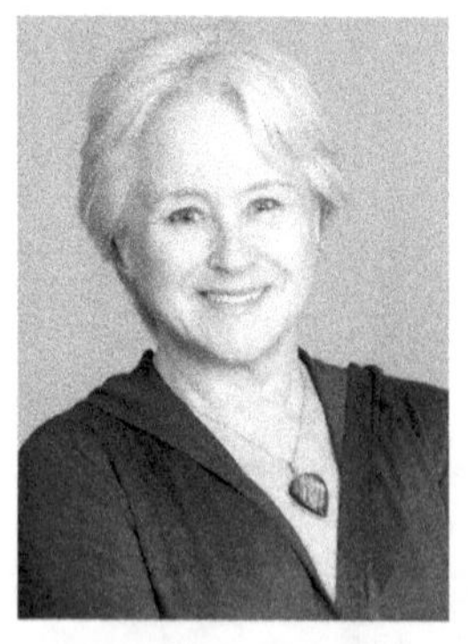

MARGUERITE JANE JONES is a business consultant, poet, speaker, and creator of The Pebbling Process™—a creative writing program that provides a process and inspiration to explore your inner storyteller. Her business and creative work is designed to assist others in finding solutions that bring the results they desire. Jane is mom to four amazing children. They are grown now and continue to amaze her. She is from Canada and now lives in Southern California.

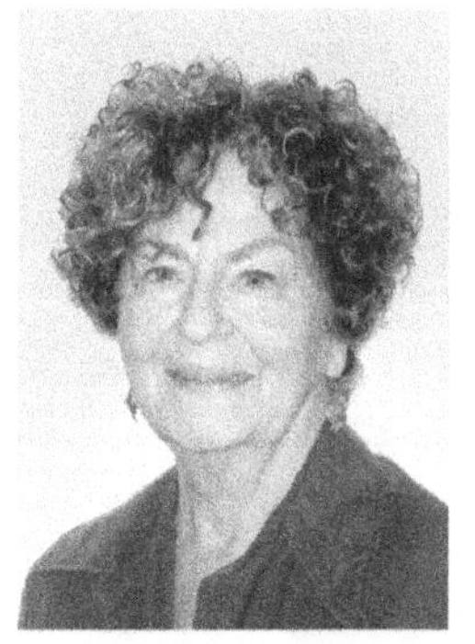 JANET HENDERSHOT is an acclaimed artist whose work has been shown across Canada; in London, England; Paris, France; San Miguel Allende, Mexico; and Bogota, Colombia. She is one of the eighteen artists who represented Canada in the XXI Olympics. Janet is the recipient of two Canada Arts Council Grants and eight Ontario Arts Council Grants. Janet was president of the Ontario Society of Artists 2005–2006 and remains as an active past president 2006–present. You can find her work at her website: www.jhendershotstudios.com

Acknowledgments

There are a number of researchers, practitioners, writers and scholars who have influenced our ways of thinking and our work. We honor their wisdom and knowledge, citing a few of them below.

Julia Cameron

Betty Edwards

Natalie Goldberg

Dr. Bruce Perry

Dr. Stephen Porges

Dr. Jim Richards

Ellen Reich

Dr. Vimala Rodgers

Dr. Stanley Rosenberg

Dr. Paul Sheele

Dr. Daniel Siegel

Brenda Ueland